# Caderno do Futuro

A evolução do caderno

# LÍNGUA INGLESA

**Book 3**
ENSINO FUNDAMENTAL

3ª edição
São Paulo - 2013

**IBEP**

Coleção Caderno do Futuro
Língua Inglesa, Book 3
© IBEP, 2013

| | |
|---:|:---|
| Diretor superintendente | Jorge Yunes |
| Gerente editorial | Célia de Assis |
| Editor | Angelo Gabriel Rozner |
| Assistente editorial | Fernanda dos Santos Silva |
| Revisão | Rachel Prochoroff |
| | Maria Inez de Souza |
| | André Odashima |
| Coordenadora de arte | Karina Monteiro |
| Assistente de arte | Marilia Vilela |
| | Nane Carvalho |
| | Carla Almeida Freire |
| Coordenadora de iconografia | Maria do Céu Pires Passuello |
| Assistente de iconografia | Adriana Neves |
| | Wilson de Castilho |
| Ilustrações | Marcos Guilherme |
| Produção gráfica | José Antônio Ferraz |
| Assistente de produção gráfica | Eliane M. M. Ferreira |
| Projeto gráfico | Departamento de Arte Ibep |
| Capa | Departamento de Arte Ibep |
| Editoração eletrônica | N-Publicações |

**CIP-BRASIL. CATALOGAÇÃO-NA-FONTE**
**SINDICATO NACIONAL DOS EDITORES DE LIVROS, RJ**

K38i
3.ed.

Keller, Victoria
   Língua Inglêsa : book 3, (8º ano) / Victoria Keller, pseudônimo dos autores Antonio de Siqueira e Silva, Rafael Bertolin. - 3. ed. - São Paulo : IBEP, 2013.
      il. ; 28 cm          (Caderno do futuro)

   ISBN 978-85-342-3570-9 (aluno) - 978-85-342-3574-7 (mestre)

   1. Língua inglesa (Ensino fundamental) - Estudo e ensino. I. Título. II. Série.

12-8685.                                CDD: 372.6521
                                        CDU: 373.3.016=111

27.11.12    03.11.12                             041072

3ª edição - São Paulo - 2013
Todos os direitos reservados.

**IBEP**

Av. Alexandre Mackenzie, 619 - Jaguaré
São Paulo - SP - 05322-000 - Brasil - Tel.: (11) 2799-7799
www.editoraibep.com.br  editoras@ibep-nacional.com.br

Reimpressão Gráfica Cromosete - Janeiro 2016

# SUMÁRIO

## CONTENTS

| | |
|:---|---:|
| GENERAL REVIEW | 4 |
| LESSON 1 – POSSESSIVE ADJECTIVES AND PRONOUNS | 15 |
| LESSON 2 – PREPOSITIONS | 24 |
| LESSON 3 – INDEFINITE PRONOUNS | 32 |
| LESSON 4 – WHY...? BECAUSE | 40 |
| REVIEW | 44 |
| LESSON 5 – OCCUPATIONS (PROFESSIONS) | 50 |
| LESSON 6 – PAST TENSE | 58 |
| LESSON 7 – DID YOU WATCH...? | 64 |
| LESSON 8 – I DID NOT WORK | 74 |
| LESSON 9 – DID YOU SLEEP WELL? | 81 |
| REVIEW | 87 |
| LESSON 10 – I DIDN'T GO TO | 92 |
| LESSON 11 – I DIDN'T TAKE | 97 |
| LESSON 12 – PERSONAL PRONOUNS | 103 |
| REVIEW | 109 |
| ADDITIONAL TEXTS | 112 |
| FUN TIME | 122 |
| LIST OF IRREGULAR VERBS | 128 |
| GENERAL VOCABULARY | 131 |

**SUBJECT**

**NAME**

**TEACHER**

| HOUR | MONDAY | TUESDAY | WEDNESDAY | THURSDAY | FRIDAY | SATURDAY | SUNDAY |
|---|---|---|---|---|---|---|---|
| | | | | | | | |
| | | | | | | | |
| | | | | | | | |
| | | | | | | | |
| | | | | | | | |
| | | | | | | | |

**TESTS AND WORKS**

# General review – books 1 and 2

1. Escreva **a** ou **an**.
   a) He is _____ American singer.
   b) She is _____ English painter.
   c) I am _____ teacher.
   d) This is _____ orange.
   e) We have _____ shop downtown.
   f) Paul is _____ intelligent boy.
   g) It's _____ interesting game.
   h) It's _____ animal.
   i) He's _____ good player.
   j) He's _____ great man.

2. Escreva as formas verbais abreviadas.
   a) I am = I'm
   b) You are =
   c) He is =
   d) She is =
   e) We are =
   f) They are =

3. Mude para o presente contínuo.

   a) The girls **plant** trees.

   b) The secretary **writes** a letter.

   c) He **studies** English.

4. Escreva em inglês.

   a) Vou ler um livro.

   b) Eles estão indo jogar tênis.

   c) Ela está lendo uma revista.

5. Faça frases usando o caso genitivo (caso possessivo).

   a) this – family – John's

   b) poems – this poet's – I like

   c) nose – The clown's – red

**6.** Leia com atenção e traduza.

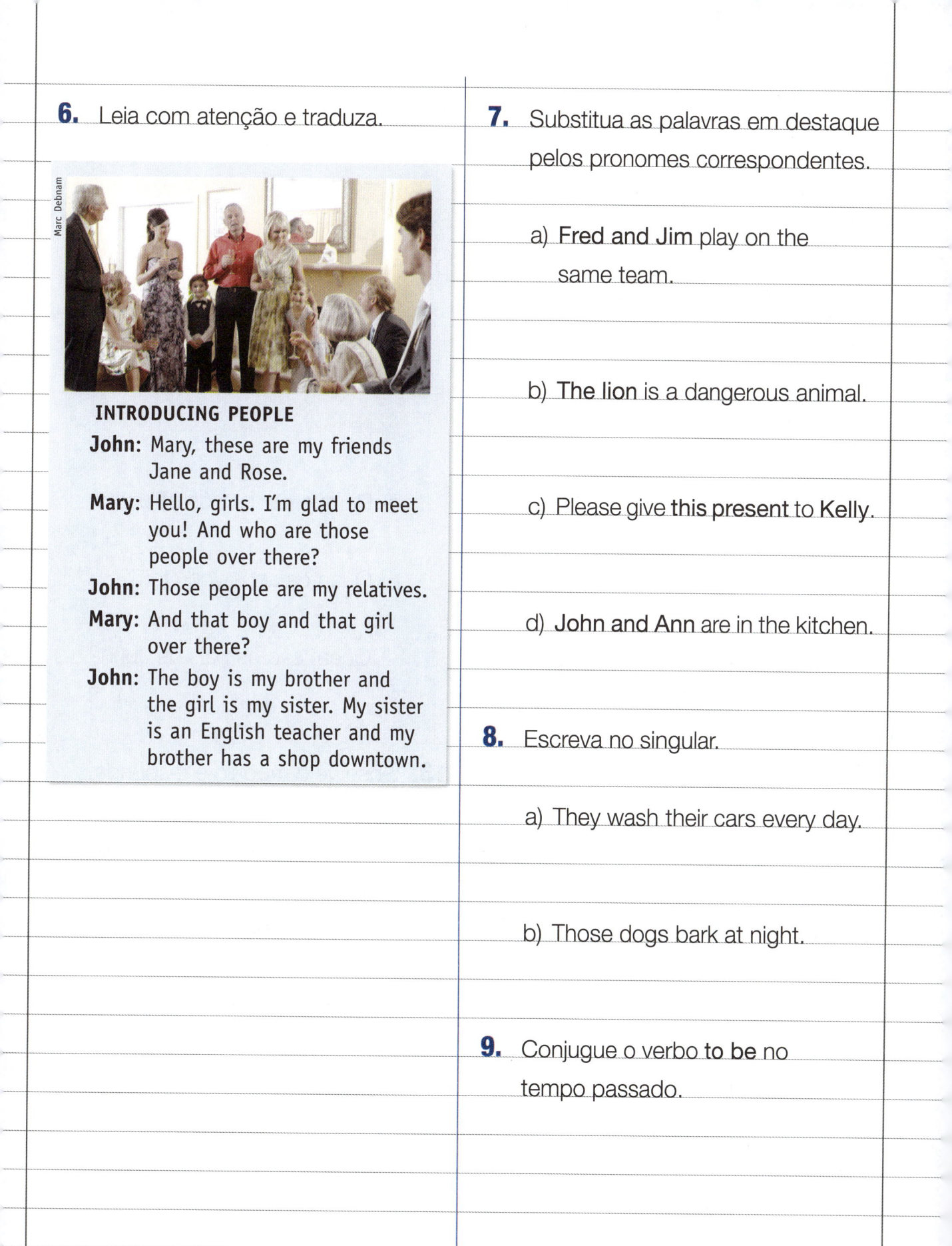

**INTRODUCING PEOPLE**

**John:** Mary, these are my friends Jane and Rose.
**Mary:** Hello, girls. I'm glad to meet you! And who are those people over there?
**John:** Those people are my relatives.
**Mary:** And that boy and that girl over there?
**John:** The boy is my brother and the girl is my sister. My sister is an English teacher and my brother has a shop downtown.

**7.** Substitua as palavras em destaque pelos pronomes correspondentes.

a) **Fred and Jim** play on the same team.

b) **The lion** is a dangerous animal.

c) Please give **this present** to Kelly.

d) **John and Ann** are in the kitchen.

**8.** Escreva no singular.

a) They wash their cars every day.

b) Those dogs bark at night.

**9.** Conjugue o verbo **to be** no tempo passado.

**10.** Escreva no plural.

a) I am a happy boy.

b) She was a beautiful girl.

c) He likes my friend.

d) You are an engineer.

**11.** Organize frases, utilizando as palavras dadas.

a) where/stamps? on the table.

b) who/those people? my friends

c) How/old/you? twelve

**12.** Escreva em inglês.

a) De onde você é?

b) Você é da Itália?

c) Nós somos brasileiros e ela é inglesa.

d) De que cor são os balões?

e) Quantos anos você tem?

f) Quem são os pais de John?

**13.** Observe o modelo e responda.

– Is your brother 10 years old?
(no, 12)
– **No, he is not. He is 12 years old.**

a) – Is Sharon at the club now?
(no, at home)

b) – Are your parents from Italy?
(no, Canada)

c) – Were your parents in Europe last year? (no, United States)

d) – Is it 8 o'clock now? (no, 9)

**14.** Observe os dados sobre Diana Rossi e responda às questões.

**DIANA ROSSI**
22 years old
Italian singer
Italian and English speaker
1,50 m tall
56 kilos
45 Italo Street
Blond hair
Brown eyes
Thin
Interests: dancing, reading, theater

About Diana Rossi.

a) What's her name?

b) What's her family name?

c) What's her first name?

d) Where is she from?

e) How old is Diana?

f) What's her occupation?

g) How many languages does she speak?

h) How tall is she?

i) How heavy is she?

j) Where does she live?

k) What's she like?

l) Does Diana like dancing?

m) Does she like going to the theater?

n) Does she speak Japanese?

**15.** Escreva **how much** ou **how many**.

a) _____ milk is there in the glass?

b) _____ cats are there in the old house?

c) _____ people are there in the shop?

d) _____ money is there in the drawer?

**16.** Mude para a forma interrogativa.

There are many people in the stadium.

**17.** Escreva no tempo passado.

There is a knife on the table.

**18.** Complete com **how old** ou **how many**.

a) _____ are you?

b) _____ cows are there in the field?

c) _____ birds can you see in the tree?

d) _____ is your friend?

**19.** Responda.

a) How old are you?
I am _____ (years old).

b) How old is your father?
He is _____ (years old).

c) How old is your mother?
She is _____ (years old).

**20.** Complete as frases com **there is** ou **there are**.

a) _____ a lot of people in the stadium.

b) _____ a goalkeeper in the goal.

c) _____ a stadium in my city.

**21.** Responda às questões.

a) How many seasons are there in a year?

b) How many months are there in a year?

c) How many weeks are there in a month?

d) How many days are there in a week?

e) How many hours are there in a day?

f) How many minutes are there in an hour?

g) How many seconds are there in a minute?

**22.** Complete as frases com **has** ou **have**.

a) We _____ a lot of musical instruments.
b) She _____ a beautiful house.
c) My father _____ many friends.
d) He _____ many tickets.
e) They _____ several books.
f) She _____ a magazine.
g) We _____ good ideas.

**23.** Escreva as frases no plural.

a) I have a good friend.

b) He has a big car.

c) You have a good teacher.

**24.** Escreva as frases no plural.

a) He is studying his lesson.

b) She is writing her name.

c) She is helping her friend.

d) I am studying my lesson.

**25.** Escreva as frases com o adjetivo possessivo **his** ou **her**.

a) I know John's mother.

b) I know Mary's son.

c) I know Meg's friend.

d) I know Jack's family.

**26.** Traduza para o português.

a) This is **John's house**.

b) This is **Betty's house**.

c) This is my **mother's garden**.

**27.** Use o caso genitivo nas frases.

a) carro de Paulo

b) boneca de Maria

**28.** Use o caso genitivo nas frases.

a) Whose pen is this? (Bob's)

b) Whose car is this? (Janet's)

**29.** Reescreva as frases no possessivo usando **'s** ou **'**.

a) The car of Mary.

b) The house of John.

c) The bar of Charles.

d) The cars of the teachers.

**30.** Use os possessivos **his** ou **her**.

a) This house belongs to Peter.

b) This car belongs to Bob.

c) That dress belongs to Jane.

d) That picture belongs to Janet.

**31.** Responda livremente.

Whose pen is this?

**32.** Escreva suas atividades diárias usando as expressões: **before school, at school, after school.**

**MY ACTIVITIES**
I get up.
I read.
I watch television.
I eat breakfast.
I draw.
I brush my teeth.
I play with my friends.
I comb my hair.
I paint.
I learn Maths.
I pay attention to the teacher.
I go home.
I do my homework.
I wash my face.
I eat dinner.
I sleep.

Before school

At school

After school

**33.** Escreva os nomes dos dias da semana em inglês. Na língua inglesa os dias da semana e os meses são escritos com letra inicial maiúscula.

**34.** Escreva as horas por extenso.

10h00

10h15

10h30

10h40

10h45

10h55

**35.** Observe os relógios e responda.

a) What time is it?

b) What time is it?

c) What time is it?

**36.** Responda às questões.

a) What is the day before Saturday? It is _____.

b) The day after Sunday is _____.

c) Saturday comes before _____.

**37.** Complete as frases com as preposições **from** e **to**.

a) He comes _____ Brazil and goes _____ Canada.

b) From Rio you may go _____ Belo Horizonte.

**38.** Traduza para o português.

I am coming from the United States.

**39.** Complete as frases com **starts** ou **start**.

a) The game _____ at nine o'clock.

b) They _____ work at seven o'clock.

**40.** Escreva as frases na forma negativa.

a) The goalkeeper could get the ball.

b) I can watch the game.

**41.** Responda na forma afirmativa. Use resposta curta (**short answer**).

a) Are you sure?

b) Can you help me?

c) Do you sleep well?

d) Does he play football?

e) Does she speak English?

f) Do you like milk?

g) Do you like cake?

**42.** Responda na forma negativa. Use resposta curta (**short answer**).

a) Are you going on vacation?

b) Can you help me?

c) Does she drive well?

d) Do you like fish?

e) Does he like soup?

f) Does she like coffee?

**43.** Escreva na forma negativa.

a) Close the door.

b) Sit down.

c) Play here.

d) Stay here, please.

**44.** Traduza para o inglês. Use **doesn't** (ou **does not**).

a) Rogério não gosta de bolo.

b) Maria não gosta de peixe.

**45.** Escreva na forma interrogativa.

a) She loves me.

b) He reads well.

c) You love me.

d) They drink juice.

**46.** Complete as frases com os verbos correspondentes.

a) He   wakes up   at 7 every morning.

b) He _____ a shower after getting up.

c) He _____ breakfast with his parents.

d) He _____ for school at about 8.

e) He _____ lunch at school.

f) He _____ home at 3.

g) He _____ his homework in the afternoon.

h) He _____ to bed at about 10.

(   ) has          (   ) goes
(   ) leaves       (   ) does
(   ) gets         ( a ) wakes up
(   ) takes        (   ) eats

# Lesson 1 – Possessive adjectives and pronouns

**Lisa:** What is your favorite rose?

**Helen:** My favorite rose is red, and yours?

**Lisa:** Mine is yellow. I like yellow roses.

**1.** Traduza o diálogo acima.

| ADJETIVOS POSSESSIVOS | | PRONOMES POSSESSIVOS | |
|---|---|---|---|
| **My** | meu, minha | **Mine** | o meu, a minha |
| **Your** | teu, tua, seu, sua | **Yours** | o teu, a tua, o seu, a sua |
| **His** | dele | **His** | o/a dele |
| **Her** | dela | **Hers** | o/a dela |
| **Its** | dele, dela (neutro) | **Its** | o/a dele, dela (neutro) |
| **Our** | nosso, nossa | **Ours** | o nosso, a nossa |
| **Your** | vosso, vossa, seu, sua, de vocês | **Yours** | o vosso, a vossa, o seu, a sua |
| **Their** | deles, delas (neutro) | **Theirs** | o/a deles, delas (neutro) |

Observe:

a) Os adjetivos possessivos estão sempre acompanhados de um substantivo.
   **My** rose is **red**. (Minha rosa é vermelha).

b) Os pronomes possessivos substituem os substantivos.
   My rose is red, and **yours**? (Minha rosa é vermelha, e a sua?)

c) Os pronomes substantivos possessivos terminam por **s**, com exceção de **mine**.

d) No emprego de **his**, **her**, **its** faça a concordância com o possuidor:

**Jack** and **his** brother.           (Jack e seu irmão.)
**Jack** and **his** sister.            (Jack e sua irmã.)
**Mary** and **her** father.            (Maria e seu pai.)
**Mary** and **her** mother.            (Maria e sua mãe.)
The **hen** and **its** food.           (A galinha e seu alimento.)

John: **Your** brother is driving a new car. Is this **his** car?
Peter: Yes, **our** father gave this car on **his** birthday.
John: Oh, nice!

**2.** Traduza o diálogo.

**3.** Passe as frases para o plural, conforme o exemplo.

This is my book.
**These are my books.**

a) This toy is mine.

b) That is our car.

c) The ruler is yours.

d) Our pencil is in the box.

e) That is her blouse.

**Observação:**
Os possessivos, em inglês, não se flexionam. Ficam com a mesma forma no singular e no plural.

**4.** Complete com **his**, **her** ou **its**.

a) Jane and _____ father work in a restaurant.

b) George is playing football with _____ friends.

c) Helen likes to dance with _____ boyfriend.

d) That is an old car; _____ door is broken.

e) She washes _____ car on Mondays.

f) He washes _____ socks every day.

g) Roy and _____ mother study at night.

h) That is an ancient church; _____ tower is very high.

**5.** Complete traduzindo os possessivos entre parênteses para o inglês. Observe o exemplo.

(Meus – os teus)
**My** pencils are black; **yours** are red.

a) (deles – o nosso)
_____ car is new; _____ is old.

b) (minha – a sua)
I like _____ house; do you like _____?

c) (dela)
Susan is in _____ bedroom.

d) (tuas)
Are these pens _____?

e) (suas – delas)
Are these magazines _____?
No, they are _____.

**6.** Preencha os espaços com possessivos, de acordo com o sujeito.

a) I wash _____ hands before the meals.
And you, do you wash _____?

b) Mary brushes _____ teeth after the meals.

c) Helen and _____ brother study in the morning.

d) You take care of _____ bag and I take care of

**7.** Escolha a alternativa correta.

a) (   ) Where are yours books?
   (   ) Where are your books?

b) (   ) It is not my ball. Mine is black.
   (   ) It is not my ball. My is black.

c) (   ) Lucy is my best friend. Who is your?
   (   ) Lucy is my best friend. Who is yours?

d) (   ) Our teacher is nice. And your?
   (   ) Ours teachers are nice. And yours?
   (   ) Our teacher is nice. And yours?

**8.** Una as duas frases num único período. Observe o exemplo.

Your mother is tall. My mother is short.
**Your mother is tall but mine is short.**

a) Our house is blue. Your house is green.

b) Your hair is short. My hair is long.

c) My bedroom is clean. Your bedroom is dirty.

d) Your girlfriend has a dog. My girlfriend has a cat.

**9.** Faça o exercício seguindo o exemplo.

(house / old)
**Is that your house?**
**No, it is not. Mine is old.**

a) (ball / red)

b) (dog / black)

c) (pen / new)

**10.** Escreva as frases seguindo o modelo abaixo.

(eyes / blue / green)
**My eyes are blue but hers are green.**

a) (hair / short / long)

b) (country / large / small)

c) (shoes / clean / dirty)

d) (English class / in the morning / at night)

**11.** Monte frases em inglês e faça a tradução para o português de acordo com o exemplo.

(Mike – dog)
**The dog belongs to Mike. It's his.**
O cão pertence a Mike. É dele.

a) (book / John)

b) (house / Mary and John)

c) (factory / Paul and Bob)

**12.** Obrserve o exemplo e traduza as frases para o idioma inglês.

Minha casa é velha,
mas a dela é nova.
**My** house is old but **hers** is new.

a) Nossa escola é moderna, mas a deles não é.

b) Sua namorada é ruiva, mas a minha é loira.

c) Os pais deles são médicos, mas os nossos são músicos.

d) Minha mãe é jovem, mas a sua não é.

e) Minha caneta é azul, mas a sua é vermelha.

f) Meu livro é fácil, mas o dele é difícil.

**13.** Assinale os possessivos no texto.

Mom: Bob, how was your first day at your new school?
Bob: Great! My teacher promised to give me a present.
Mom: A present?!
Bob: Yes. When I arrived he pointed to a chair in the corner and said: "Please sit over there for the present".

Qual é a melhor tradução da última frase?
( ) Sente-se ali para ganhar um presente.
( ) Sente-se ali por enquanto.

## POSSESSIVE PRONOUNS

Veja o boxe abaixo e responda às perguntas a seguir.

**Silvia Borelli**
Singer
Birthday on the next Sunday.
From Italy – Italian
35 North Avenue
Interests: music, watch TV.

**John Brown**
Football player
Birthday in July
From England – English
59 Nelson Square
Interests: football, horse riding.

**Rose Oliveira**
Actress
Birthday in April
From Brazil – Brazilian
59 Tiradentes Street
Interests: music, watch TV, theater.

Responda de acordo com os dados acima.

**14.** About Silvia Borelli

a) What's her first name?

b) What's her family name?

c) Where is she from?

d) When is her birthday?

e) What's her occupation?

f) What's her address?

g) What are her interests?

**15.** About Rose Oliveira.

a) What's her last name?

b) When is her birthday?

c) What's her nationality?

d) What's her occupation?

e) Is music one of her interests?

**16.** About John Brown.

a) What's his family name?

b) Is he a football player?

c) What are his interests?

d) What is his birth country?

**17.** Escreva (true) ou (false) de acordo com os dados do quadro.

a) (          ) Silvia's birthday is on the next Saturday.
b) (          ) John's interests are football and horse riding.
c) (          ) Silvia's birth country is Brazil.
d) (          ) Rose's occupation is playing football.
e) (          ) Rose likes theather, Silvia likes music and John, football.

**18.** Assinale os possessivos no texto. Depois, traduza-o usando o vocabulário no final do livro.

A problem
Carol wants to cover the floor of her bedroom with a carpet.
Her bedroom is 4 meters long and 3 meters wide.
To know the area of her bedroom you must multiply the lenght by the width:
4 x 3 = 12 m². Her bedroom is twelve square meters.
How much is she going to pay for the carpet of her bedroom, if one square meter costs 7 dollars?
It's very easy to solve:
multiply 7 by 12 = 84.
She is going to pay eighty-four dollars for the carpet for her bedroom.

**ANOTAÇÕES**

## Dictation

**19.** Ouça com atenção o ditado que o professor vai apresentar e escreva.

**ANOTAÇÕES**

# Lesson 2 – Prepositions

The sun is shinning behind the mountains.

The car is in front of the house.

**1.** Traduza os textos acima.

**2.** Observe o quadro de preposições e relacione com a sua tradução.

( 1 ) near     ( ) ao longo de
( 2 ) along     ( ) sobre
( 3 ) on     ( ) perto de
( 4 ) with     ( ) dentro, em
( 5 ) in     ( ) com
( 6 ) through     ( ) fora de
( 7 ) out of     ( ) através
( 8 ) into     ( ) para dentro, dentro
( 9 ) beyond     ( ) além de

**3.** Preencha os espaços com as preposições **between, before, from, to, by, in front of** e **without**.

a) November comes December.

b) November is October and December.

c) I go _____ school in the morning.

d) She is coming _____ Brasilia.

e) There is a garden _____ my house.

f) Brazil is far _____ England.

g) I go to school _____ bus.

h) I can't buy the ball _____ money.

**4.** Observe a figura e complete as lacunas com as preposições **behind, on, under** e **in front of**.

What can you see in the picture?
I can see:
a) A man _____ the truck.
b) A boy _____ the truck.
c) A cat _____ the truck.
d) A dog _____ the truck.

**5.** Responda.

a) Who is in front of the truck?

b) Who is behind the truck?

**6.** Ligue as preposições antônimas.

| | |
|---|---|
| in | under |
| near | out |
| over | far from |
| behind | after |
| before | with |
| without | in front of |
| inside | outside |

**7.** Escreva frases antônimas, usando as preposições do boxe abaixo. Observe o exemplo.

> behind – outside – inside – from
> out of – in front of – before – far from
> (going) to – (coming) from

The children are playing **inside** the house.

The children are playing **outside** the house.

a) The bird was **outside** the cage.

b) The bicycle is **behind** the car.

c) I live **near** you.

d) I am going **to** New York.

e) The cat is jumping **into** the box.

f) We are going to the club **after** lunch.

g) Is the bus station **far from** here?

h) Is the school **in front of** the church?

i) Is she **going to** Rio?

j) Are the teachers **inside** the room?

**8.** Escolha no quadro as preposições corretas e preencha as lacunas. Observe o exemplo.

> by – from – on – with – to
> along – in

George usually goes to work **by** car.

a) They are coming _____ Rio _____ plane.

b) Please put this book _____ the table.

c) Please put these pencils _____ their box.

d) The program _____ TV last night was very good.

e) I don't like to travel _____ train.

f) She is opening the door _____ a key.

g) _____ money we buy a lot of things.

h) Are you going _____ Curitiba? No, I'm going _____ Porto Alegre.

i) I am driving _____ Jefferson Avenue.

**9.** Traduza as preposições e complete a cruzadinha.

1) com:
2) em:
3) debaixo de:
4) fora:
5) longe de:
6) sem:
7) atrás de:

EMPREGO DAS PREPOSIÇÕES: **IN, ON, AT**

1) Com relação a lugar (**Where...?**)
   a) Usa-se **in** com relação a
      países: Roger lives **in** England.
      estados: Silvia lives **in** Pernambuco.
      cidades: Fernando lives **in** Brasília.
      bairros: Robert lives **in** Pinheiros district.
   b) Usa-se **on** com relação a nomes de ruas:
      Mary lives **on** Oliver Street.
   c) Usa-se **at** diante de nomes de ruas com números:
      Paul lives **at** 45 Palm Street.

2) Com relação a tempo (**When...?**)
   a) Usa-se **in** diante de anos:
      Jane was born **in** 1994. (nineteen ninety-four)

      meses: Lucy was born **in** May.
      estações do ano: **In** the spring.

   b) Usa-se **on** diante de datas e dias da semana:
      Paul was born **on** April first.
      Paul was born **on** the first of April.
      We go to the park **on** Sundays.

   c) Usa-se **at** diante de horas e datas comemorativas:
      The class begins **at** eight o'clock.

**10.** Responda às perguntas, usando devidamente as preposições in, on, at.

a) Where do you live, Fred?
   (England)

b) Where do you live, Mônica?
   (Brazil)

c) Where do you live, Jessica?
   (Pernambuco)

d) Where does George live?
   (Oliver Street)

e) Where does she work?
   (25 Palm Street)

**11.** Responda às perguntas, usando devidamente as preposições in, on, at.

a) When were you born? (1994)

b) Where do you live?
   (Spring Street)

c) When is your birthday, Julie?
   (May)

d) When is your birthday, Robert?
   (March, 10th)

e) When is the next show?
   (9 o'clock)

**12.** Escolha a preposição mais adequada e complete as frases.

a) We are talking _____ you.
   (above – about)

b) She was not _____ home.
   (at – in)

c) I wash my hands _____ meals. (at – before)

d) May comes _____ April.
   (before – after)

e) I am _____ John and Mary in this photo. (at – between)

f) The class begins _____ eight o'clock. (at – in)

g) There is someone _____ the door. (under – at)

h) Write your name _____ the top of the page. (over – at)

i) I work _____ a bank. (on – in)

**13.** Desenhe algumas situações em que seja possível usar as preposições abaixo. Feitos os desenhos, invente uma frase com essas preposições.

> between – behind – in front of – near –
> far from – beside – through

**14.** Reescreva as frases, substituindo as preposições em destaque por outras de sentido oposto. Observe o exemplo abaixo.

I am **going to** Bahia.
I am **coming from** Bahia.

a) She lives **far from** my house.

b) The pencils are **out of** the box.

c) I do my homework **without** your help.

d) There is a garden **behind** the house.

**15.** Complete traduzindo as preposições dos parênteses.

a) Where are the pencils? (sobre)
   They are _____ the table.

b) Where is Mary? (dentro)
   She is _____ her bedroom.

c) Where are your friends? (na)
   They are _____ school.

d) Where is Sue? (com)
   She is _____ Jane.

e) Where are my shoes? (debaixo)
   They are _____ the bed.

f) Where are you from? (de origem)
   I'm _____ England.

g) When is your birthday? (em)
   It is _____ August.

**16.** Riddles. Solucionar o enigma.

a) When does Thursday come before Wednesday?

### CANDIDO PORTINARI

Candido Portinari was born in Brodowski, in the state of São Paulo, in 1903. He was son of Italian immigrants. Portinari died in Rio, in 1962.

Among his famous works is *War and Peace*.

*War and Peace* is a large mural in the United Nations building, in New York. Portinari painted that mural from 1952 to 1956. It was a gift from the Brazilian government to the seat of the United Nations Organization.

**17.** Releia o texto e responda.

1. When was Portinari born?

2. Where was he born?

3. When did he die?

**18.** Underline the prepositions in the text.

### I WAS BORN IN BLUMENAU

I was born in Blumenau in the state of Santa Catarina on the 10th of May in 1980.

Now I live in Rio de Janeiro in front of the beach of Copacabana.

I work for an American company.

I sometimes go to a movie theater, usually at seven o'clock.

In December, in the summer, I go home to visit my family in Blumenau. From Blumenau we go to the beaches in Florianopolis to enjoy the waves of the sea.

After that, in the everning, we go to a restaurant with our friends, near the famous Hercilio Luz bridge.

# Lesson 3 – Indefinite pronouns

**What do you prefer:**
To have **little** money and **a lot of** friends, or to have **a lot of** money and **few** friends?

**I prefer to have a lot of money and few friends.**

**INDEFINITE PRONOUNS** (PRONOMES INDEFINIDOS)

**Much**: muito, muita.
**Little**: pouco, pouca.

Observe:

a) Usa-se **much** e seu antônimo **little** para as coisas que não se contam:
   **much** time: muito tempo;
   **little** time: pouco tempo.

b) Geralmente não se usa **much** em frases afirmativas ou interrogativas. Nesse caso, usa-se a expressão **a lot of**.
   The English drink **a lot of** tea. (Os ingleses bebem muito chá).

**Many**: muitos, muitas.
**Few**: poucos, poucas.

Usa-se **many** e seu antônimo **few** para seres/objetos contáveis:
**many** books: muitos livros;
**few** girls: poucas meninas.

**1.** Traduza o diálogo acima.

**2.** Complete as frases com os indefinidos **much, little, many, few, a lot of**, de acordo com as indicações.

> I am coming from the supermarket with **few** things...

a) Mary spends _____ time cleaning the house. (muito)

b) I don't have _____ time. (muito)

c) Do you have _____ time to sleep? (muito)

d) Mr Brian is a famous doctor. He has _____ patients. (muitos)

---

**a little**: um pouco (Usa-se diante de coisas não contáveis: água, suco, leite...)
**a few**: poucos (Usa-se diante de seres/ objetos contáveis: maçãs, carros, pessoas...)

---

**3.** Traduza as falas dos balões.

**Going shopping**

> I am going to the supermarket with **a lot of** money!

**4.** Complete as lacunas com **a little** ou **a few**.

a) The bus leaves in _____ minutes. Hurry up!

b) – How much ice cream do you want?
– Just _____, please.

c) – How many dollars do you have?
– Just _____ dollars... one, two, three dollars.

33

d) My father gives me _____ money every weekend.

e) – Do you want some more coffee?
– Yes, please, but just _____.

> **much = a lot of:** muito, uma porção de (Usado diante de coisas não contáveis, como água, açúcar, tempo, atenção…)
>
> **many = a lot of = lots of, plenty of:** muitos, uma porção de (Usado diante de objetos e seres contáveis como frutas, livros, alunos…)

**5.** Preencha as lacunas com os indefinidos do boxe acima.

a) I drink _____ water during the day.

b) She can't buy the present because she doesn't have _____ money.

c) There are _____ birds in the Amazon forest.

d) When I am hungry I eat _____ rice and beans.

e) I don't like _____ sugar in my coffee.

f) We can see _____ stars in the sky at night.

g) There are _____ American soldiers fighting in Afeganistan.

h) _____ students don't pay attention in class.

**6.** Complete com **much, little, many** e **few**. Observe o exemplo.

Twenty cars: **many** cars
Two cars: **few** cars

a) Atlantic ocean: _____ water
A glass of water: _____ water

b) A bank: _____ money
A purse: _____ money

c) A tennis match: _____ players
A football game: _____ players

**7.** Substitua os indefinidos em negrito por seus antônimos. Veja o exemplo.

She drinks **a lot of** tea.
She drinks **little** tea.

a) He usually takes **little** coffee.

b) There isn't **much** water in this lake.

c) Do you have **many** friends?

d) There were **few** people in the room.

**8.** Traduza para o português.

a) I don't like much salt on the salad.

b) We have little time to do our exercises.

c) There were few fruit in the basket.

d) How many people were there in the party?

e) How much money do you have in your pocket?

**9.** Complete com o pronome certo.

a) There are _____ pencils in the box.
(little / few / much)

b) How _____ boys are there in your class?
(much / many / little)

c) I have _____ money but a lot of friends.
(a lot of / little)

**10.** Assinale as alternativas corretas e complete as frases.

a) How _____ shoes are there in the shop windows?
( ) much ( ) many ( ) few

b) To learn how to drive a car requires _____ patience and practice.
( ) a lot of ( ) much ( ) little

## INDEFINITES

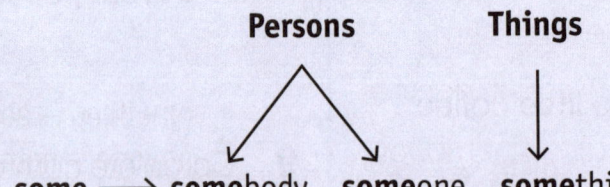

**Persons** → **some**body, **some**one  
**Things** → **some**thing

some → somebody, someone, something

São usados em frases alternativas.

There are **some** boys in the class. → Há alguns meninos na classe.
There is **some** water in the glass. → Há alguma água no copo.
There is **somebody** in the car. → Há alguém no carro.
There is **someone** in the car. → Há alguém no carro.
There is **something** in the box. → Há alguma coisa na caixa.

**People** → **any**body, **any**one
**Things** → **any**thing

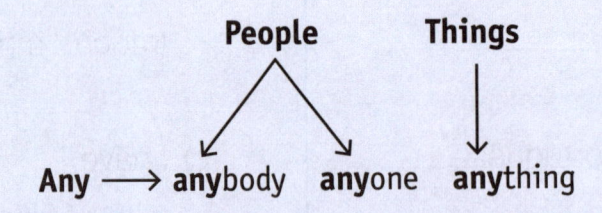

Any → anybody, anyone, anything

São usados em frases interrogativas e também em frases negativas, com a negação **not**.

I **don't** know **anybody**.

Is there **any** money in the box?

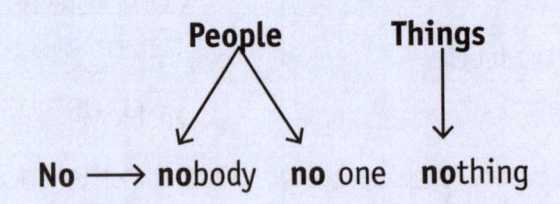

**People** → **no**body, **no** one
**Things** → **no**thing

No → nobody, no one, nothing

Is there **any** water in the glass? → No, there isn't **any**.
Há alguma água no copo? → Não, não há nenhuma.
Is there **anybody** in the house? → No, there isn't **anybody**.
Há alguém na casa? → Não, não há ninguém.
Is there **anything** in the box? → No, there isn't **anything**.
Há alguma coisa na caixa? → Não, não há nada.
There is **nobody** in the room. → There is **nothing** in the box.
Não há ninguém na sala. → Não há nada na caixa.

**11.** Preencha com **few** ou **little**.

a) _____ friends   e) _____ milk
b) _____ water    f) _____ doctors
c) _____ books    g) _____ money
d) _____ cars     h) _____ apples

**12.** Responda às perguntas na forma afirmativa e depois na negativa. Observe o exemplo.

Do you have any coffee?
**Yes, I have some.**
**No, I don't have any.**

a) Do you have any money?

b) Do you have any work to do?

c) Do you have any friends?

d) Is there any fruit in the basket?

**13.** Complete as frases com os pronomes indefinidos abaixo.

> something – some – anybody
> anyone – nothing – nobody

a) What are you going to do _____ on Sunday?

b) Can _____ tell me the capital of Canada?

c) I have to do _____ to help her.

d) The film was in Japanese, so I didn't understand _____ they said.

e) I'm sad because _____ remembered my birthday.

f) I don't want _____ to eat.

g) Do you have _____ to say?

h) I know _____ about painting. Can you tell me about _____ famous painters?

**14.** Preencha com **some** ou **any**.

a) I have _____ friends that are artists.
b) I don't know _____ painter.
c) We gave _____ suggestions.
d) Do you have _____ friends in Rio?
e) There are _____ good news in this newspaper.
f) I'm learning _____ new words in English.

**15.** Complete as frases e a cruzadinha com **some**, **any** e seus compostos.

1) There is _____ knocking at the door.
( ) anybody ( ) somebody

2) It's too dark. I can't see _____ .
( ) something ( ) anything

3) Do you have _____ money?
No, I don't have _____ .
( ) any ( ) some

4) I have _____ money for you.
( ) some ( ) anything

5) I want to tell you _____ about your job.
( ) some ( ) something

6) _____ people do not think before speaking.
( ) any ( ) some

7) Do you have _____ suggestion?
( ) some ( ) any

8) Is there _____ interested on pictures?
( ) somebody ( ) anybody

## Dictation

**16.** Ouça com atenção o ditado que o professor vai apresentar e escreva.

**ANOTAÇÕES**

## Lesson 4 – Why...? Because...

– **Why** are you running?
– **Because** I am late!

Usamos a palavra interrogativa **why** em perguntas, e **because** em respostas.

**1.** Traduza o diálogo.


**2.** Una as perguntas às respostas mais adequadas.

| | |
|---|---|
| Why are you sad? | Because I am late. |
| Why are you late? | Because she abandoned me. |
| Why are you sleeping? | Because I am happy. |
| Why are you smiling? | Because I missed the bus. |
| Why are you running? | Because I am sick. |
| Why are you eating? | Because I am tired. |
| Why are you going to the doctor's? | Because I am thirsty. |
| Why are you drinking water? | Because I am hungry. |

**3.** Dê uma resposta em português para as seguintes perguntas.

a) Why are there wars and violence in the world?

b) Why is there little food for millions of people?

c) Do you know why there are corrupt politicians?

**4.** Siga o exemplo e responda.

Why are you running? (I am late.)
I am running because I am late.

a) Why is the baby crying?
   (He is hungry.)

b) Why are you sad?
   (My father is angry with me.)

c) Why are you so happy?
   (My girlfriend loves me.)

**5.** Ligue as frases.

a) Why are you taking so many pills? •   • Because I need money to live.

b) Why are you running? •   • Because I am sick.

c) Why are you working? •   • Because I am late.

> **Why** pode vir acompanhado da palavra **not**, o que significa "por que não?".
> Observe o exemplo:
> – Do you want to go to Rio with us?
>   (Você deseja ir ao Rio conosco?)
> – No, I don't.
>   (Não, não quero.)
> – **Why not**? (Por que não?)

**6.** Siga o exemplo.

– Are you going to buy a car?
  (It is too expensive.)
– No, I'm not.
– Why not?
– Because it's too expensive.

a) – Are you going to play football?
     (I have homework to do.)

b) – Is she going to the party tonight? (She is sick.)

c) – Can you tell me the time? (My watch is broken.)

**7.** Traduza os seguintes diálogos.

a) – Do you like to eat?
– Yes, I do.
– Do you like to work?
– No, I don't.

b) – Do you like to read?
– Yes, I do.
– Do you like to write?
– No, I don't.

c) – Do you like to hug?
– Yes, I do.
– Do you like to kiss?
– Yes, I do.

d) – Do you like to travel?
– Yes, I do.
– Do you like to drive?
– No, I don't. I like to travel by bus.

**8.** Complete os diálogos abaixo.

a) – Do you like fish?
– No,
– Do you like spinach?
– No,
– What do you like then?
– I like

b) – Do you like music?
– Yes,

– Do you like to dance?
– No,

c) – Does she like coffee?
– No,
– Does she like tea?
– Yes,

d) – Do you want to play football?
– No,
– What do you want to play?
– I want to play

e) – Do your parents listen to the radio?
– No,
– Do they like watching television?
– Yes,
– How about you?
– I hate

f) – Do you like pears?
– No,
– Do you like apples?
– Yes,

g) – Do you like me?
– Yes,
– Do you like Peter?
– No,

**9.** Riddle. Why is the letter T like an island?

**10.** Você costuma fazer perguntas a si mesmo sobre o mundo que o cerca? Pessoas conscientes de seu papel no mundo vivem questionando tudo. Veja algumas perguntas e depois faça as suas, em inglês.
– Why is the sky blue?
– Why to get vaccinated?
– Why do I have to eat salad and fruit?
– Why are so many people homeless?
– Why are there so many languages in the world?
– Why do heavy airplanes stay up in the air?
– Why are some people black and others white?

# Review – Lessons 1, 2, 3 and 4

**1.** Complete com **do** ou **does**.

a) What time _____ Ben get up?

b) When _____ he play football?

c) When _____ Mary and John go to school?

d) What _____ you like to eat?

e) Where _____ she work?

f) Why _____ you go to the club every day?

g) Why _____ she study in this school?

**2.** Preencha as lacunas com **do**, **does**, **don't** ou **doesn't**.

a) _____ Milton believe in ghosts?

b) Milton _____ believe in ghosts.

c) _____ this computer work?

d) _____ they help you?

e) _____ your father help you?

f) _____ your friend work in a factory?
Yes, he _____
No, he _____

g) _____ you like ice cream?
Yes, I _____
No, I _____

h) _____ your parents live here?
Yes, they _____
No, they _____

**3.** Use **why** ou **because**.

a) _____ are you running? _____ I am very late.

b) I am happy _____ I have many friends.

**4.** Traduza os diálogos para o inglês.

a) – Por que você está trabalhando?

44

– Porque eu preciso de dinheiro.

b) – Por que você está cantando?

– Porque eu estou feliz.

**5.** Preencha com **many** ou **much**.

a) _____ women
b) _____ money
c) _____ people
d) _____ water
e) _____ time
f) _____ teeth

**6.** Preencha as lacunas, escrevendo, em inglês, as palavras em destaque.

a) **Há muitas** crianças no parque.
_____ children in the park.

b) **Havia poucas** mulheres na sala.
_____ women in the room.

c) **Havia muito** açúcar no café.
_____ sugar in the coffee.

d) **Há pouco** açúcar no café?
_____ sugar in the coffee?

e) **Havia poucos** alunos na sala de aula?
_____ students in the classroom?

**7.** Preencha as lacunas com **few** ou **little**.

I drink _____ coffee; just a _____ cups a day.

**8.** Substitua as palavras em negrito pelos pronomes possessivos. Observe o exemplo.

That house is **her house**.
That house is **hers**.

a) Those magazines are **my magazines**.

b) That purse is **her purse**.

c) Is this dog **his dog**?

d) Is that ball **your ball**?

e) No, it's not **my ball**. It's

f) Is that table **our table**?

g) Are those books **your books**?

h) That house is **their house**.

i) This pen is not **my pen**.

j) This wallet is not **my wallet**.

**9.** Complete as frases com adjetivos possessivos.

a) Peter usually goes to school with _____ sister.

b) I enjoy _____ History classes very much.

c) Jane and _____ brother study in the same class.

d) Paul and Mary do _____ homework together.

e) _____ first name is Richard.

f) Mrs Gates loves _____ children very much.

g) Most parents love _____ children.

h) Do you do _____ homework in the morning?

i) Mary is writing a letter to _____ parents.

j) Bob and Jim don't like _____ country.

k) Mary is wearing _____ new dress.

l) I always help _____ mother at home.

**10.** Observe as figuras e preencha corretamente os balões com as falas a seguir.

- She doesn't like rock music.
- Why not?
- I don't know.

- Why didn't you study the lesson?
- Because it was impossible. My friends played rock music all night!

**11.** Observe as figuras e complete as frases com as preposições out, in, with, without, between, among.

Come _____, please!

Get _____!

George is _____ Natalie and Nicole.

This singer is _____ fans.

**12.** Complete com as preposições at, in, of, to, from.

a) The children are going _____ school.
b) The students are coming _____ school.
c) John works _____ an office.
d) I get up _____ seven every day.
e) I go to school _____ the morning.
f) I have breakfast _____ seven thirty every day.
g) Wait a moment. I come back _____ a minute.
h) They are coming back _____ Salvador tomorrow.
i) I want a glass _____ milk.
j) The legs _____ the table are broken.
k) I was born _____ August.
l) My parents live _____ Curitiba.
m) My parents live _____ 45 Tiradentes street.
n) They were _____ home yesterday.
o) My class begins _____ eight o'clock.
p) Are the pencils _____ the box?
q) Where are you from?
   I'm _____ Bahia.

**13.** Copie as sentenças embaixo das imagens correspondentes.

a) Who's this man? He's Mr Brown. He's a worker.
b) Who's this woman? She's Mary. She's a teacher.
c) Who's this man? He's John. He's a cyclist.
d) Who's this man? He's Paul. He's a doctor.
e) Who's this man? He's Peter. He's a fisherman.

**A LEADER**

When Martin Luther King Jr received the Nobel Prize, in December 1964, he said:

"I accept the Nobel Prize for Peace at a moment when twenty-two million African Americans of the United States of America are engaged in a creative battle to end the long night of racial injustice.

I accept this award in behalf of a civil rights movement which is moving to establish a reign of freedom and a rule of justice".

**14.** Leia o texto e responda às questões.

a) Who received the Nobel Prize for Peace?

b) When did he receive the Nobel Prize?

c) How many African Americans were engaged in a battle to end the racial injustice?

# Lesson 5 – Occupations (professions)

– Richard, what do you want to be in the future?
– I want to be a pilot.
– A pilot? Why?
– Because I like airplanes. I always dream that I am in a big airplane flying over the world.
– And you, Jessica? What do you want to be?
– I want to be a nurse. I like to take care of unhealthy people.
– Very well, Jessica.

**1.** Traduza o diálogo acima sobre profissões, utilizando o vocabulário do fim do caderno.

**2.** Consulte o quadro abaixo e responda às perguntas. Observe o exemplo.

**PLACES**
at the fishmonger's   at the library
at the butcher's      at the drugstore
at the greengrocer's  at the stationary story
at the bookshop
at the newsstand      at the store
at the toyshop        at the hospital
at the jewelry store  at the doctor's
at the bakery         at the chemist's

Where can you buy bread?
**At the bakery.**

a) Where can you buy meat?

b) Where can you buy newspapers and magazines?

**I can buy newspapers and magazines at the newsstand.**

c) Where can you buy fruit and vegetables?

d) Where can you buy fish?

e) Where can you buy jewels?

f) Where can you buy books?

g) Where can you buy toys?

h) Where can you buy papers, pencils, pens?

i) Where can you buy medicines?

j) Where can you read books, and magazines?

k) Where can you eat and drink?

l) Where can you go when you are sick?

**3.** Assinale a alternativa certa.

a) Who builds houses?
( ) the doctor
( ) the engineer
( ) the player

b) Who paints pictures?
( ) the cook
( ) the nurse
( ) the artist

c) Who lives on a farm?
( ) the singer
( ) the farmer
( ) the doctor

d) Who works in a factory?
   (　) the worker
   (　) the sailor
   (　) the reporter

e) Who plays football?
   (　) the nurse
   (　) the secretary
   (　) the football player

f) Who works in a hospital?
   (　) the farmer
   (　) the singer
   (　) the doctor and the nurse

**4.** Ligue os profissionais aos seus respectivos trabalhos.

The cook　　　　•　　•　cuts hair
The dentist　　　•　　•　cooks food
The policeman　•　　•　treats our teeth
The hairdresser •　　•　teaches
The teacher　　•　　•　makes furniture
The carpenter　•　　•　catches criminals

**5.** Observe o exemplo e responda às perguntas.

Who catches criminals? (policeman)
**The policeman catches criminals.**

a) Who treats our teeth? (dentist)

b) Who works in an office? (clerk)

c) Who cuts women's hair? (hairdresser)

d) Who makes furniture? (carpenter)

e) Who looks after our health? (doctor)

f) Who builds buildings? (engineer)

g) Who paints pictures? (artist)

h) Who works in a library? (librarian)

i) Who commands soldiers? (officer)

**6.** Competição sobre profissões.

Os alunos, dois a dois, jogam o dado, e, conforme o número que cair, alternadamente, um pergunta e o outro responde. Se não souber responder, volta ao início do jogo, na posição **Start**. Antes de começar o jogo, leiam várias vezes a lista de profissões abaixo e depois cubram com uma folha o quadro de respostas **occupations**.

- **Start**
- **1** Who sells bread?
- **2** Who sells meat?
- **3** Who sells vegetables?
- **4** Who paints pictures?
- **5** Who makes furniture?
- **6** Who teaches English?
- **7** Who works in a farm?
- **8** Who works in a ship?
- **9** Who sells jewels?
- **10** Who plays football?
- **11** Who sells fish?
- **12** Who works in a library?
- **13** Who sells fruit?
- **14** Who sells newspapers?
- **15** Who cuts women's hair?
- **16** Who treats our teeth?
- **17** Who commands soldiers?
- **18** Who catches criminals?
- **19** Who sells medicines?
- **20** Who cooks in a restaurant?
- **21** Who looks after our health?
- **22** Who sells books?
- **Finish**

**OCCUPATIONS**
football player – fishmonger – librarian – jeweller – farmer – sailor – policeman – dentist officer – baker – greengrocer – butcher – carpenter – artist – English teacher newsagent – hairdresser – chemist – doctor – bookseller – cook

**7.** Preencha a cruzadinha e as frases empregando as palavras do quadro abaixo.

| | | |
|---|---|---|
| newspapers (jornais) | books (livros) | pens (canetas) |
| fish (peixe) | bread (pão) | flowers (flores) |
| meat (carne) | medicine (remédios) | vegetables (legumes) |

1. The newsagent sells...
2. The butcher sells...
3. The florist sells...
4. The bookseller sells...
5. The chemist sells...
6. The baker sells...
7. The greengrocer sells fruit and...
8. The stationery store sells paper and...
9. The fishmonger sells...

**8.** Complete a cruzadinha empregando as palavras do quadro abaixo para responder às perguntas.

> greengrocer (verdureiro)
> florist (florista)
> newsagent (jornaleiro)
> bookseller (livreiro)
> butcher (açougueiro)
> jeweller (joalheiro)
> chemist (farmacêutico)
> stationery store (papelaria)
> baker (padeiro)
> fishmonger (vendedor de peixe)

1. Who sells magazines and newspapers?
2. Who sells bread?
3. Who sells meat?
4. Who sells jewels?
5. What kind of store sells paper and pens?
6. Who sells flowers?
7. Who sells books?
8. Who sells fruit and vegetables?
9. Who sells fish?
10. Who sells medicines?

**9.** Responda às perguntas.
Observe o exemplo abaixo.
What does a dentist do?
**He treats our teeth.**

a) What does a cook do?

b) What does a carpenter do?

c) What does a hairdresser do?

d) What does an electrician do?

e) What does an artist do?

f) What does a clerk do?

g) What does a librarian do?

h) What does an engineer do?

i) What does a policeman do?

**10.** Responda às perguntas.
Observe o exemplo abaixo.
Where does a clerk work? (office)
**He works in an office.**

a) Where does a librarian work? (library)

b) Where does a cook work? (restaurant)

c) What does a dentist treat? (teeth)

d) What does a hairdresser cut? (women's hair)

e) What does an engineer build? (houses, bridges...)

f) What does a carpenter make? (furniture)

g) What does an electrician repair? (electrical apparatus)

## Dictation

**11.** Ouça com atenção o ditado que o professor vai apresentar e escreva.

**ANOTAÇÕES**

# Lesson 6 – Past tense

## PAST TENSE

(TEMPO PASSADO: PRETÉRITO PERFEITO E IMPERFEITO DE VERBOS REGULARES.)

*In Rio, we visited our parents and then walked along Copacabana beach. At four o'clock we traveled to São Paulo by bus. We arrived here at about ten o'clock and watched a film on TV.*

**PAST TENSE OF REGULAR VERBS** (TEMPO PASSADO DE VERBOS REGULARES)

**I visited:** eu visitei (tempo passado)
**We walked:** nós caminhamos (tempo passado)
**They traveled:** eles viajaram (tempo passado)
**We arrived:** nós chegamos (tempo passado)

Os verbos em destaque acima estão no tempo passado (**past tense**).

Forma-se o **past tense** dos verbos regulares acrescendo-se **ed** ou **d** aos verbos na sua forma básica:    visit → visit**ed**
                                                        arrive → arrive**d**

Observe a conjugação do verbo **to visit** (visitar) no **past tense**:

I visited (eu visitei/visitava)          We visited (nós visitamos/visitávamos)
You visited (você visitou/visitava)      You visited (vocês visitaram/visitavam)
He visited (ele visitou/visitava)        They visited (eles visitaram/visitavam)
She visited (ela visitou/visitava)

## Observações:

Verbos regulares terminados em **y** precedido de vogal fazem o **past tense** acrescentando-se **ed** (to **play** – **played**). Quando o **y** é precedido de consoante, o **past tense** termina em **ied** e o **y** sai (to **study** – **studied**).

**1.** Observe os exemplos e escreva os verbos no **past tense**.

(terminado em vogal)
to invite (convidar): **invited**
to dance (dançar):
to like (gostar):
to live (viver, morar):
to love (amar):
to complete (completar):
to move (mudar):

(terminado em consoante)
to invent (inventar):
to want (querer):
to look (olhar):
to reach (conseguir):
to help (ajudar):
to wash (lavar):
to clean (limpar):
to play (jogar):
to cross (cruzar):
to plant (plantar):

(y precedido de **consoante**)
to study (estudar): **studied**
to copy (copiar):
to carry (carregar):
to occupy (ocupar):
to hurry (apressar):
to cry (gritar, chorar):
to try (tentar):

(y precedido de **vogal**)
to play (jogar): **played**
to stay (ficar):
to employ (empregar):
to delay (atrasar):

**2.** Conjugue no **past tense** os verbos.

a) To stay (ficar)
I
You
He/She
We
You
They

b) To cry (gritar)
I
You

He/She
We
You
They

c) To love (amar)
I
You
He/She
We
You
They

**3.** Escreva no **past tense**.
Observe o exemplo.

Mary cleans the house.
**Mary cleaned the house.**

a) They live on a farm.

b) I study in the morning.

c) He plays football in Europe.

d) You help my friend.

e) My father works in a factory.

**4.** Reescreva as frases, passando os verbos para o tempo passado, substituindo ou acrescentando as circunstâncias de tempo entre parênteses. Observe o exemplo.

My maid **cleans** my bedroom every day. (yesterday)
My maid **cleaned** my bedroom **yesterday.**

a) She **works** as a secretary. **(last year)**

b) I **help** my mother in the kitchen. **(last week)**

c) I **wash** my car on Saturdays. **(last Saturday)**

d) The thief **attacks** her in the street. **(last night)**

e) We **play** football on Sundays.
   (last Saturday)

f) I **learn** English at school.
   (last year)

**5.** Reescreva o texto abaixo no tempo passado. Substitua a expressão **every day** por **yesterday**.

> Bob arrives in his office at eight o'clock every day.
> He works from eight o'clock a.m. to five o'clock p.m. and then he returns home. He helps his wife in the kitchen and after dinner they talk and watch TV programs.

**6.** Traduza o texto anterior no tempo passado.

**7.** Responda com o verbo auxiliar **to be** no passado. Observe o exemplo.

Where were you last night?
(at home)
**I was at home.**

a) Where were you yesterday?
   (at school)

b) Where were your parents yesterday morning?
   (at the supermarket)

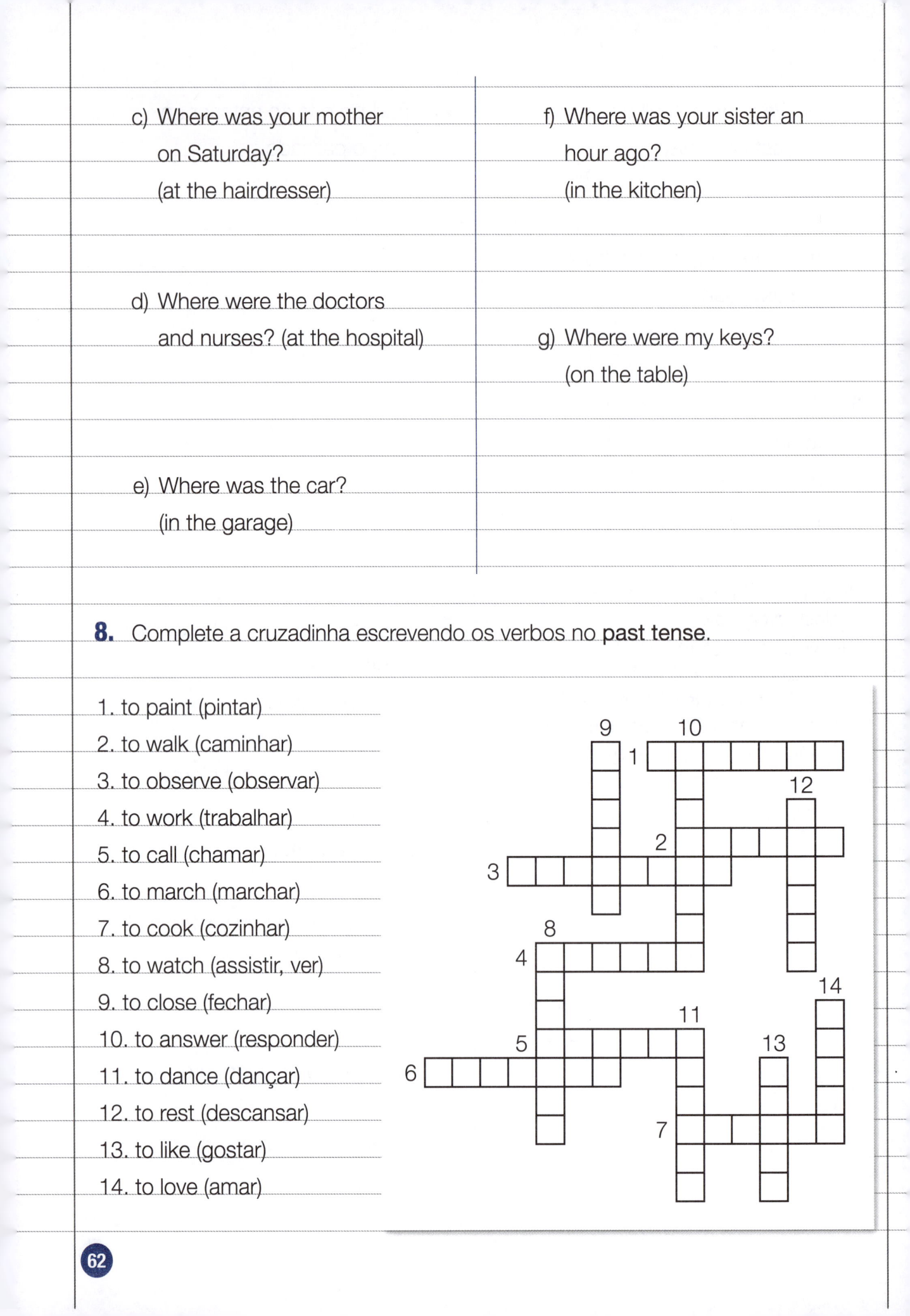

c) Where was your mother on Saturday? (at the hairdresser)

d) Where were the doctors and nurses? (at the hospital)

e) Where was the car? (in the garage)

f) Where was your sister an hour ago? (in the kitchen)

g) Where were my keys? (on the table)

**8.** Complete a cruzadinha escrevendo os verbos no **past tense**.

1. to paint (pintar)
2. to walk (caminhar)
3. to observe (observar)
4. to work (trabalhar)
5. to call (chamar)
6. to march (marchar)
7. to cook (cozinhar)
8. to watch (assistir, ver)
9. to close (fechar)
10. to answer (responder)
11. to dance (dançar)
12. to rest (descansar)
13. to like (gostar)
14. to love (amar)

**9.** Complete as frases com os verbos no passado. Observe o exemplo.

(to rain) It rained a lot yesterday.

a) (to receive - to smile)
   The child _____ the present and _____ .

b) (to wait)
   We _____ for you for hours.

c) (to promise)
   She _____ to help me.

d) (to work)
   My father _____ at night last year.

e) (to search)
   We _____ for information at the tour agency.

f) (to watch)
   My friends _____ an interesting film last night.

**ANOTAÇÕES**

# Lesson 7 – Did you watch...?

– Do you like to watch films?

– Yes, I do.

– Did you watch *Romeo and Juliet*?

– Yes, I did. It's a marvelous film about love between two young people. It's an exciting love story. Romeo and Juliet lived in Verona, in Italy.

## FORMA INTERROGATIVA DO TEMPO PASSADO
### (EMPREGO DA FORMA AUXILIAR DID)

Sempre que fizermos perguntas no tempo passado com verbos não auxiliares, devemos usar **did** para todas as pessoas do verbo.

Observe a conjugação do verbo **to like** (gostar) no tempo passado, na forma afirmativa e na interrogativa:

**To like – past tense**

| Affirmative form | Interrogative form |
|---|---|
| I liked | Did I like...? (Eu gostei...?) |
| You liked | Did you like...? (Você gostou...?) |
| He/She liked | Did he/she like...? (Ele/Ela gostou...?) |
| We liked | Did we like...? (Nós gostamos...?) |
| You liked | Did you like...? (Vocês gostaram...?) |
| They liked | Did they like...? (Eles gostaram...?) |

### Observação:

Para transformar frases afirmativas em interrogativas, com verbos não auxiliares, no tempo passado, siga o esquema:

**did** + sujeito + verbo na forma básica
(infinitivo sem **to**)

did + you + watch *Romeo and Juliet*?

(Você assistiu a *Romeu e Julieta*?)

**1.** Traduza o diálogo acima.

**2.** Siga o exemplo e passe para a forma interrogativa.

They worked on Sundays.
**Did they work on Sundays?**

a) She invited you to the party.

b) Jim lived in London last year.

c) You cleaned the house today.

d) He washed the car last week.

e) They moved to Recife last year.

f) You played tennis at the club.

g) She helped her friend.

h) Mary studied in the same school.

i) You copied all the exercises.

j) She stayed in front of the school.

k) They answered all the questions.

l) You painted your house last year.

m) She planted flowers last spring.

**3.** Siga o exemplo e ordene as palavras e forme frases interrogativas no tempo passado.

live / did / your family / farm / on / a
**Did your family live on a farm?**

a) football / play / did / Sundays / on / they

b) she / did / in / a / work / toyshop

c) move / to / another / town / they / did

d) well / your / team / play / did

e) she / wash / her / clothes / did

f) you / like / her / did

**4.** Assinale as frases corretas.

a) ( ) Did she worked on Sundays?
   ( ) Did she work on Sundays?
   ( ) Did she works on Sundays?

b) ( ) Does they like you?
   ( ) Does they liked you?
   ( ) Does she like you?

c) ( ) Did she play football?
   ( ) Did she plays football?
   ( ) Did she played football?

d) ( ) Do they studied at night?
   ( ) Do they study at night?
   ( ) Do they studies at night?

**5.** Releia o começo da lição anterior sobre o **past tense** dos verbos regulares. Complete as frases, colocando os verbos entre parênteses no tempo passado. Observe o exemplo.

(to start) The football game **started** at four o'clock.

a) (to brush) I _____ my teeth after dinner.
b) (to wash) My father _____ the plates after dinner.
c) (to walk) We _____ in the park last Sunday.
d) (to learn) I _____ a lot of words in English yesterday.
e) (to work) They _____ until ten o'clock last night.
f) (to move) She _____ to São Paulo last month.
g) (to plant) We _____ some flowers last spring.

**6.** Complete as frases com verbos do boxe abaixo.

> to celebrate – to call – to enter
> to water – to watch

a) They _____ the room an hour ago.
b) Lucy _____ the plants yesterday morning.
c) My sister _____ her birthday last month.
d) After dinner we _____ TV.
e) Yesterday I _____ the doctor because I was not well.

**7.** Mude as frases do tempo presente para o tempo passado, usando as expressões adverbiais entre parênteses. Observe o exemplo.

The shop opens at 8 o'clock every day. (yesterday)
**The shop opened at 8 o'clock yesterday.**

a) I visit my parents on the weekends. (last week)

b) Mary cleans her room every morning. (last week)

c) We study English every day. (last month)

d) We wash the car every weekend. (yesterday morning)

**8.** Passe os verbos do tempo presente para o tempo passado, usando as expressões entre parênteses. Observe o exemplo.

They work here on Sundays. (last year)
**They worked here on Sundays last year.**

a) I live in Brazil. (in 1995)

b) She studies English in England. (last year)

c) Janice cleans her house every day. (yesterday)

d) I wash my car on Saturdays. (last week)

e) They move to Rio this week. (last month)

f) We play football on Sundays. (last Saturday)

g) We study in the same school. (last year)

**9.** Observe o exemplo e redija as perguntas no tempo passado usando a palavra interrogativa **when** e o auxiliar **did**.

**When did you clean the house?**
I cleaned the house yesterday morning.

a) 
   I opened the window an hour ago.

b) 
   I arrived yesterday morning.

c) 
   I washed my car last week.

d) 
   I painted the house last year.

e) 
   She planted the flowers last month.

**10.** Observe o exemplo e faça perguntas no tempo passado.

The football game started at 4 o'clock.

**Did the football game start at 4 o'clock?**

a) You brushed your teeth after dinner.

b) Your father washed the plates after dinner.

c) The girls walked in the park yesterday.

d) She learned many new words last year.

e) They worked until 10 o'clock last night.

f) They moved to San Francisco last year.

g) Mary planted some flowers last month.

**11.** Observe o exemplo e faça perguntas no tempo passado.

Mary cleaned the room yesterday morning.
**When did Mary clean the room?**

a) Bob washed the car last Saturday.

b) They visited their parents last weekend.

c) The Oliveiras moved to San Francisco last year.

d) Lucy watered the plants yesterday morning.

e) Jane celebrated her birthday last month.

**12.** Observe o exemplo e responda às perguntas.

When did the school open?
(at 8 o'clock)
**The school opened at 8 o'clock.**

a) When did the Oliveiras move to San Francisco? (last year)

b) When did Lucy water the plants? (yesterday morning)

c) When did Jane celebrate her birthday? (last month)

d) When did you visit your parents? (last month)

e) When did the football game start? (at 4 o'clock)

f) When did you brush your teeth? (after dinner)

g) When did Yone plant flowers? (last week)

**13.** Assinale a alternativa correta.
A forma interrogativa dos verbos não auxiliares no tempo passado obedece ao seguinte esquema.

( ) Do + sujeito + forma básica do verbo
( ) Does + sujeito + forma básica do verbo
( ) Did + sujeito + forma básica do verbo

**Observação:**
Forma básica – verbo no infinitivo sem a partícula **to**.
to work → forma básica: **work**
to invite → forma básica: **invite**

**14.** Complete com **do**, **does** ou **did**, de acordo com a tradução das interrogativas. Observe o exemplo.

**Did** they go to the park?
Eles foram ao parque?

a) _____ you get up early?
(Você se levanta cedo?)

b) _____ she work in a pet shop?
(Ela trabalha numa loja de animais de estimação?)

c) _____ they help you?
(Eles ajudaram você?)

d) _____ Flavia love John?
(Flavia ama John?)

e) _____ you study at night?
(Você estudava à noite?)

f) _____ you go to school by bus?
(Você vai para a escola de ônibus?)

g) _____ she like coffee or tea?
(Ela gosta de café ou de chá?)

h) _____ the children watch TV last night?
(As crianças assistiram a TV na noite passada?)

i) _____ your sister live in Porto Alegre?
(Sua irmã mora em Porto Alegre?)

j) _____ you speak English?
(Você fala inglês?)

k) _____ she invite you to the party?
(Ela convidou você para a festa?)

l) _____ she like you?
(Ela gosta de você?)

**15.** Observe o exemplo e faça perguntas no tempo passado.

I cleaned my house. (you)
**Did you clean your house, too?**

a) I lived in São Paulo last year. (she)

b) She worked in a drugstore. (you)

c) I liked her. (you)

d) The girls danced well. (the boys)

e) I answered all the questions. (you)

f) I studied at night. (they)

g) I visited my parents last month. (you)

**16.** Traduza as frases, ultilizando as palavras entre parênteses. Observe o exemplo.

Você fala inglês.
(English / you / speak)
**You speak English.**

a) Você fala inglês?
(English / you / do / speak)

b) Ela fala inglês.
(English / speaks / she)

c) Ela fala inglês?
(English / she / speak / does)

d) Ela gostava de mim.
(me / liked / she)

e) Ela gostava de mim?
(me / like / she / did)

**17.** Assinale a alternativa correta.

a) ( ) Usa-se **does** em frases interrogativas, na 3ª pessoa do singular do presente simples.
   ( ) Usa-se **does** em frases interrogativas no plural.
   ( ) O plural de **do** é **does**.

b) ( ) As frases interrogativas, em inglês, geralmente começam por **do, does** ou **did**.
   ( ) Usa-se **do** ou **does** em frases interrogativas no tempo passado.
   ( ) Usa-se **did** em frases interrogativas no tempo presente.

c) Quando fazemos perguntas com **do, does** ou **did**, o verbo principal fica com a forma:
   ( ) do passado
   ( ) do futuro
   ( ) do infinitivo (sem o **to**)

> **Observação:**
> **SHORT ANSWER**
> Na **short answer** (resposta curta), as formas auxiliares **do, does, did** da resposta têm o mesmo significado do verbo principal da pergunta.

**18.** Observe o exemplo e dê respostas curtas afirmativas.

– Did you like the story?
– **Yes, I did.**
   (– Sim, eu gostei.)

a) – Did she clean the house?

b) – Did you get up early?

c) – Did they work yesterday?

d) – Did Mary help her brother?

e) – Did the shops open last Sunday?

f) – Did Mary invite you to the party?

g) – Did you like the film?

h) – Did the boys play football?

**19.** Faça perguntas no tempo passado e depois responda, como no exemplo.

Where - she - to work - last year / in a toy shop.
**Where did she work last year?**
**She worked in a toy shop.**

a) How long - you - to stay in that city / for two weeks.

b) How many times - the teacher - to explain - the same lesson / three times.

c) What time - she - to call - you / at 7 o'clock.

d) What - the students - to study yesterday / History.

e) What - she to want to tell you / a secret.

## Dictation

**20.** Ouça com atenção o ditado que o professor vai apresentar e escreva.

# Lesson 8 – I did not work

– Did you work yesterday?

– No, **I did not work** yesterday.

– Why not?

– Because I do not work on Saturdays.

## FORMA NEGATIVA DO TEMPO PASSADO
### (EMPREGO DA FORMA AUXILIAR **DID NOT** OU **DIDN'T**)

Sempre que quisermos negar no tempo passado, com verbos não auxiliares, devemos usar **did not** ou **didn't** para todas as pessoas do verbo.

Observe a conjugação do verbo **to work** (trabalhar) forma negativa, no tempo passado:

**To work – Past Tense, negative form**

I did not work.
I didn't work. (Eu não trabalhei.)

You did not work.
You didn't work. (Você não trabalhou.)

He, she, it did not work.
He, she, it didn't work. (Ele, ela não trabalhou.)

We did not work.
We didn't work. (Nós não trabalhamos.)

You did not work.
You didn't work. (Vocês não trabalharam.)

They did not work.
They didn't work. (Eles não trabalharam.)

1. Traduza o diálogo da página anterior.

> **Atenção:**
> Deixe o verbo principal na forma infinitiva sem a partícula **to**.

2. Conjugue o verbo **to dance** (dançar) na forma negativa, no **past tense** (tempo passado). Observe o exemplo.

**Full form** (forma por extenso)
I **did not dance**.
(Eu não dancei.)
You
(Você não dançou.)
He/She
(Ele/ela não dançou.)
We
(Nós não dançamos.)
You
(Vocês não dançaram.)
They
(Eles/elas não dançaram.)

**Contracted form** (forma contraída)
I              dance.
You            dance.
He/She         dance.
We             dance.
You            dance.
They           dance.

3. Observe os exemplos e complete as frases com **don't**, **doesn't** ou **didn't**, de acordo com a tradução.

I **don't** like football.
(Eu não gosto de futebol.)

She **doesn't** like football.
(Ela não gosta de futebol.)

My parents **didn't** like football.
(Meus pais não gostavam de futebol.)

a) They _____ work yesterday.
   (Eles não trabalharam ontem.)

b) She _____ clean the house.
   (Ela não limpa a casa.)

c) The bus _____ stop here.
   (O ônibus não para aqui.)

d) The goalkeeper _____ catch the ball.
   (O goleiro não pegou a bola.)

e) We _____ visit our parents last week.
   (Nós não visitamos nossos pais na semana passada.)

75

f) They _____ speak English.
   (Eles não falam inglês.)

**4.** Reescreva as frases, passando para a forma negativa. Observe os exemplos.

They live on a farm. (to live)
**They do not live on a farm.**

She lives on a farm. (to live)
**She does not live on a farm.**

Mr Benson lived on a farm. (to live)
**Mr Benson did not live on a farm.**

a) I study in the afternoon. (to study)

b) She likes meat. (to like)

c) Mary answered all the questions. (to answer)

d) My team played well. (to play)

e) They speak English. (to speak)

f) My friend goes to school by bus. (to go)

g) The maid cleans the house on Mondays. (to clean)

h) I like him. (to like)

**5.** De acordo com as perguntas, dê respostas negativas no tempo presente ou no tempo passado. Observe os exemplos.

Do you speak English?
**No, I don't.**
(Não, eu não falo.)

Does she like you?
**No, she doesn't.**
(Não, ela não gosta.)

Did the children study the lesson?
**No, they didn't.**
(Não, elas não estudaram.)

a) Do you get up early?

b) Did you like the film?

c) Does she help you?

d) Did they invite you to the party?

e) Does she play football?

f) Did you read the book?

g) Does she love him?

h) Did you understand the problem?

i) Do you know England?

**6.** Assinale a resposta correta.

a) Do you work on Sundays?
( ) No, they don't.
( ) Yes, I do.
( ) Yes, you do.

b) Did they live on a farm?
( ) No, they live.
( ) Yes, they lives.
( ) No, they didn't.

c) Did she move to Minas?
( ) No, she doesn't.
( ) No, she don't.
( ) No, she didn't.

d) Does she wash the car?
( ) Yes, she washed the car.
( ) Yes, she washes the car.
( ) Yes, she wash the car.

e) Do you work in a shop?
( ) Yes, I do.
( ) Yes, I did.
( ) No, I did not.

f) Did they copy the exercises?
   ( ) Yes, they copies
        the exercises.
   ( ) Yes, they copied
        the exercises.
   ( ) Yes, they copy the exercises.

g) Do you like her?
   ( ) Yes, I liked her.
   ( ) Yes, I do.
   ( ) No, she doesn't

**7.** Responda negativamente. Observe o exemplo.

Did she dance with you last night? (my cousin)
**No, she didn't.**
**She danced with my cousin.**

a) Did you study Geography yesterday? (Science)

b) Did they play football last Saturday? (basketball)

c) Did Jane visit her parents last month? (her aunt)

d) Did you call your friend yesterday? (my mother)

e) Did you answer all the questions? (only one)

f) Did you invite your schoolmates to the party? (my friends)

**8.** Reescreva as frases conforme o exemplo.

I liked to work with John. (Meg)
**I liked to work with John but I didn't like to work with Meg.**

a) I liked to play football. (tennis)

b) She liked to study Geography. (Mathematics)

c) They liked to go to the beach. (club)

d) She liked to sing. (dance)

**9.** Consulte o vocabulário no boxe abaixo e forme frases negativas no tempo passado.

---

**WORD BANK**

**team**: time
**play**: jogar
**well**: bem
**bus**: ônibus
**yesterday**: ontem
**mother**: mãe
**clean**: limpar
**house**: casa
**wash**: lavar
**help**: ajudar
**watch**: assistir
**last night**: a noite passada
**pay**: pagar
**bill**: conta
**love**: amar
**her**: seu, dela

---

a) Meu time não jogou bem ontem.

b) Minha mãe não limpou a casa.

c) Susie não lavou seu carro. (carro dela)

d) Eles não me ajudaram.

e) Nós não assistimos à TV na noite passada.

f) Mônica não pagou a conta.

g) Jeff não amava Lisa.

**10.** Reescreva as frases, passando para a forma interrogativa.

a) Mrs. Campbell knew the answer.

b) Kelly wore her new dress to the interview.

c) Her parents let her study in the United States.

d) George lent five hundred dollars to Carol.

e) His dog bit my friend yesterday.

f) They spent the whole day on the beach.

g) They went to Venice in their honeymoon.

h) She fell down the stairs.

**ANOTAÇÕES**

# Lesson 9 – Did you sleep well?

– Jessica, did you sleep well last night?

– Yes, I slept very well, mom.

– What time did you get up?

– I got up at seven, took a shower, had a nice breakfast and went to work.

## PAST TENSE OF IRREGULAR VERBS

São considerados verbos irregulares todos aqueles que, no **past tense** (tempo passado) ou **past participle** (particípio passado), não terminam em **ed**.

## VERBOS IRREGULARES

É importante que você aprenda os verbos irregulares de cor nas suas três formas (infinitivo, passado e particípio passado), sem o que se torna impossível falar inglês. Sempre que precisar, consulte a tabela de verbos irregulares no final deste caderno. Nesta lição, procure aprender os que seguem:

| Infinitive | Past tense | Past participle |
|---|---|---|
| To meet (encontrar pessoas) | met | met |
| To take (pegar, levar, tomar) | took | taken |
| To speak (falar) | spoke | spoken |
| To understand (compreender) | understood | understood |
| To see (ver) | saw | seen |
| To read (ler) | read | read |
| To write (escrever) | wrote | written |
| To eat (comer) | ate | eaten |
| To sleep (dormir) | slept | slept |

1. Traduza o texto "Did you sleep well?".

2. Mude as frases para o **past tense**. Consulte a tabela de verbos irregulares no fim do caderno. Observe o exemplo.

   I have some friends.
   **I had some friends.**

   a) They go to school by bus.

   b) I meet my friends at school.

   c) She takes the bus in front of her house.

   d) The president speaks to the reporters in English.

   e) I understand your explanation.

3. Complete a cruzadinha, escrevendo os verbos no **past tense**.
   1. to go (ir)
   2. to read (ler)
   3. to write (escrever)
   4. to speak (falar)
   5. to eat (comer)
   6. to take (pegar, levar)
   7. to see (ver)
   8. to sleep (dormir)
   9. to understand (entender)
   10. to meet (encontrar)
   11. to have (ter)

**4.** Observe os exemplos e mude as frases para a forma interrogativa.

They speak English.
(Eles falam inglês.)
**Do they speak English?**
**(Eles falam inglês?)**

She speaks English. (Ela fala inglês.)
**Does she speak English?**
**(Ela fala inglês?)**

The president spoke in English.
(O presidente falou em inglês.)
**Did the president speak in English?**
**(O presidente falou em inglês?)**

a) They go to the park.
   (Eles vão ao parque.)

b) Mary goes to the park.
   (Mary vai ao parque.)

c) The girls went to the park.
   (As meninas foram ao parque.)

d) The monkeys eat banana.
   (Os macacos comem banana.)

e) The monkey eats banana.
   (O macaco come banana.)

f) She meets her friends at school.
   (Ela encontra as amigas dela na escola.)

g) Paula met her teacher yesterday.
   (Paula encontrou a professora dela ontem.)

**5.** Leia a tradução e escreva as frases na forma interrogativa.

a) Você lê jornais?
   (to read/read/read)

b) Ela lê jornais?

c) Você leu o jornal?

d) Você vê seus amigos nos fins de semana? (to see/saw/seen)

e) Ele vê sua namorada nos finais de semana?

f) Você viu o carro de Diana?

g) Você leva suas compras para casa? (to take/took/taken)

h) Ela leva o filho dela para casa?

i) Ele tomou o remédio ontem?

j) Eles se encontram em sua casa hoje? (to meet/met/met)

k) Ela encontra você hoje?

l) Ela encontrou a amiga dele ontem?

**6.** Escolha a alternativa correta de acordo com a tradução.

a) Ela pega o ônibus em frente à escola?
(to take /took /taken)
(   ) Does she takes the bus in front of the school?
(   ) Does she took the bus in front of the school?
(   ) Does she take the bus in front of the school?

b) Eles falam inglês bem?
(to speak/spoke/spoken)
(   ) Does they speak English well?
(   ) Do they speak English well?
(   ) Do they speaks English well?

c) O rato comeu todo o queijo?
   (to eat/ ate /eaten)
   ( ) Do the mouse eat all the cheese?
   ( ) Did the mouse ate all the cheese?
   ( ) Did the mouse eat all the cheese?

**7.** Responda às perguntas afirmativamente. Observe o exemplo.

Did you go to the club?
(to go/went/gone)
(Você foi ao clube?)
Yes, I did. (Sim, eu fui.)
I went to the club. (Eu fui ao clube.)

a) Did you speak English?
   (to speak/spoke/spoken)

b) Did you sleep well?
   (to sleep/ slept/slept)

**8.** Observe o exemplo e dê respostas negativas.

Do you sleep in class?
No, I don't.
I don't sleep in class.

a) Does she sleep in class?

b) Did they sleep in class?

c) Do you go to school?

d) Does Helen go to school?

e) Did your friend go to school?

f) Did you understand the problem?

g) Do you have a pen?

h) Does she get up early?

i) Do they read newspapers?

j) Did they take the bus?

**9.** Reescreva as frases na forma interrogativa.

a) You go to the club on Sundays.

b) She goes to school on Mondays.

c) Bob went to the supermarket.

d) She goes to school by bus.

e) You speak English.

f) They saw you at the movies.

g) John ate a big sandwich.

h) Helen wrote a long letter to you.

i) Erica took your book.

j) The mouse ate all the cheese.

k) Marcia meets her friends at school.

**ANOTAÇÕES**

# Review – Lessons 5, 6, 7, 8 and 9

1. Escreva ( R ) para os verbos regulares e ( I ) para os irregulares.

   a) to work – worked ( ) (trabalhar)
   b) to see – saw ( ) (ver)
   c) to live – lived ( ) (morar, viver)
   d) to stay – stayed ( ) (ficar)
   e) to have – had ( ) (ter)
   f) to use – used ( ) (usar)

2. Complete as frases usando os verbos no passado.

   a) I _____ Mary yesterday. (to see)
   b) Paul and Mary _____ to school in the morning. (to go)
   c) I _____ breakfast at 7. (to have)
   d) She _____ to me in English. (to speak)
   e) They _____ in the library. (to be)
   f) She _____ at home. (to be)
   g) They _____ the books from the shelf. (to take)

3. Escreva as frases no passado. Observe o exemplo.

   I work hard in the country.
   I worked hard in the country.

   a) I live in a city.

   b) They stay at home all the time.

   c) They believe in God.

   d) The dogs bark all night long.

   e) The horse jumps the fence.

   f) I study in the morning.

   g) I try to understand you.

   h) The men carry the bags.

i) The baby cries because he is hungry.

j) The teacher simplifies the test.

k) He loves her.

**4.** Observe o exemplo e continue empregando o passado dos verbos.

Did the father work hard?
**Yes, he did. He worked hard.**

a) Did he call his mother?

b) Did he return home by bus?

c) Did the mother kiss her son?

d) Did they talk for some minutes?

e) Did the mother cook the meal?

f) Did she prepare a nice salad?

g) Did they wash the dishes?

h) Did they watch a film?

**5.** Escreva na forma interrogativa. Observe o exemplo.

John worked hard yesterday.
**Did John work hard yesterday?**

a) He arrived on time yesterday.

b) He returned home by bus last Saturday.

c) She prepared a nice salad.

d) You washed the dishes.

e) They watched the film last night.

**6.** Escreva na forma negativa. Observe o exemplo.

They worked hard.
**They did not work hard.**
**They didn't work hard.**

a) I liked the film.

b) We invited John yesterday.

c) She washed the dishes.

d) She cooked last Sunday.

**7.** Crie frases usando o **past tense** dos verbos irregulares. Siga o modelo e use livremente os dados sugeridos ou outros à sua escolha.

Escolha um sujeito para o verbo, por exemplo: **he, she, they, John, Mary** etc. Escolha um complemento para o verbo, por exemplo: **a singer, a dentist, engineer** etc.

Modelos de frases:

to become / became a singer.
**They became singers.**
**She became a dentist.**
**He became an engineer.**
**John and Mary became doctors.**

a) Begin/ began to study/ at eight o'clock, at seven...
(he, she, they, you, Ted and Bob, the boys etc.)

b) buy /bought a car, a house, a skateboard, a TV set, books etc.
(he, she, they, my parents, my father, my brother etc.)

c) eat/ate a sandwich, some meat, cheese, potatoes, some fruit, some bread etc.
   (he, she, they, the girls etc.)

d) drink/ drank orange juice, lemonade, water, coke etc.
   (he, she, they, the children, my friends etc.)

**8.** Traduza o texto.

Nancy and Jeff
Nancy and Jeff went to the movies yesterday. They saw an interesting film. It started at 8 o'clock and finished at 10. They liked the film very much.
After the film they walked to a restaurant. They wanted to eat something. Jeff ordered a sandwich and Nancy a piece of cake. They both drank soft drinks. After that Nancy and Jeff walked to the parking lot near the restaurant, took their car and went home.

## Dictation

**9.** Ouça com atenção o ditado que o professor vai apresentar e escreva.

**ANOTAÇÕES**

# Lesson 10 – I didn't go to...

**John:** Mary, did you go to Rose's birthday party yesterday?
**Mary:** No, I did not go.
**John:** Did your brother and sister go?
**Mary:** No, they didn't.
**John:** Why not?
**Mary:** We went to visit our grandmother. She wasn't well. And you? What did you do yesterday? Did you go to the club?
**John:** No, I didn't. I had so much homework to do.

## VERBOS IRREGULARES NO TEMPO PASSADO – NEGATIVE FORM

A forma negativa, no tempo passado, com verbos não auxiliares, segue o esquema:

Sujeito + **did not** + forma básica do verbo

I  did not/didn't  go  to the club.
(Eu  não  fui  ao clube.)

### Verb to go – past tense – negative form

I did not go./I didn't go.
(Eu não fui.)

You did not go./You didn't go.
(Você não foi.)

He/she/it did not go. He/she/it didn't go.
(Ele/Ela não foi.)

We did not go./We didn't go.
(Nós não fomos.)

You did not go./You didn't go.
(Vocês não foram.)

They did not go./They didn't go.
(Eles/Elas não foram.)

**1.** Traduza o diálogo entre John e Mary.

**2.** Conjugue o verbo **to forget** no tempo passado.

**3.** Conjugue o verbo **to forget** no tempo passado da forma negativa, por extenso e abreviada.

APRENDA MAIS ALGUNS VERBOS IRREGULARES

| Infinitive | Past Tense | Past Participle | |
|---|---|---|---|
| To go | went | gone | (ir) |
| To begin | began | begun | (começar) |
| To bring | brought | brought | (trazer) |
| To forget | forgot | forgotten | (esquecer) |
| To drink | drank | drunk | (beber) |
| To give | gave | given | (dar) |
| To get | got | got/gotten | (conseguir) |
| To leave | left | left | (deixar, partir) |
| To make | made | made | (fazer) |
| To send | sent | sent | (enviar) |
| To pay | paid | paid | (pagar) |

**4.** Complete a cruzada escrevendo os verbos no tempo passado e a seguir ligue-os às suas respectivas traduções.

1) to go                fazer, fabricar
2) to drink             enviar, mandar
3) to make              trazer
4) to send              ir
5) to bring             beber
6) to give              começar
7) to forget            dar
8) to begin             esquecer
9) to understand        conseguir
10) to get              compreender, entender

**5.** Reescreva as frases no **past tense**, fazendo as devidas modificações.

a) The class begins at 7.

b) The football game begins at four o'clock.

c) Every day Jane brings her son to school.

d) I forget your name.

e) Every day I drink two bottles of water.

f) She gives me a lot of presents.

g) We get there by bus.

h) We leave at five o'clock.

i) Every day I send e-mails to my friends.

**6.** Escreva as frases seguindo o exemplo abaixo.

The class began at 7. (at 8)
Did the class begin at 7?
**No, the class didn't begin at 7.**
**The class began at 8.**

a) You brought my books. (copybooks)
Did you bring my books?

b) Mary forgot my first name. (last name)
Did Mary forget my first name?

c) She drank water. (orange juice)
Did she drink water?

d) You got a motorcycle. (a car)
   Did you get a motorcycle?

e) They left for Rio.
   (Santa Catarina)
   Did they leave for Rio?

f) He made modern furniture.
   (nice toys)
   Did he make modern furniture?

g) You sent letters. (postcards)
   Did you send letters?

**7.** Responda às perguntas, usando os verbos no **past tense**. Observe o exemplo abaixo.

Did you bring my books? (yesterday)
**Yes, I brought your books yesterday.**

a) When did the class begin? (at seven o'clock)

b) When did the football game begin? (at four o'clock)

c) When did she leave for Rio? (at nine o'clock)

d) Where did you get these magazines? (at the newsstand)

e) How much did you pay for the magazines? (seven dollars)

# Lesson 11 – I didn't take...

Leia com atenção os diálogos a seguir.

– Hi Jane! Where did you go yesterday?
– I went to shopping, but I **didn't** buy a gift for Julia.
– Why not?
– Because I **didn't** find anything interesting.

– John, why are you sad?
– Oh, Mom! I **didn't** go to school yesterday and my team lost the game.
– You were sick.
– I know, but my team **didn't** win the championship.

**IRREGULAR VERBS – PAST TENSE – NEGATIVE FORM**

A forma negativa dos verbos não auxiliares segue o esquema:

Nome ou pronome + do not/don't / does not/doesn't / did not/didn't + verbo na forma básica

Observe o exemplo:
I bought a skateboard. (Eu comprei um skate.)
I did not buy a skateboard. (Eu não comprei um skate.)

Para se obter a forma negativa, com verbos regulares e irregulares, usamos **do not/don't** ou **does not/doesn't** para o presente e **did not/didn't** para o passado. Devemos, porém, ter o cuidado de deixar o verbo principal na sua forma básica. (Obtém-se a forma básica suprimindo a partícula **to** do infinitivo.

Exemplo: to find: encontrar/forma básica: find.

## APRENDA MAIS ALGUNS VERBOS IRREGULARES:

| Infinitive | Past Tense | Past Participle |
|---|---|---|
| To know (saber, conhecer) | knew | known |
| To buy (comprar) | bought | bought |
| To steal (roubar) | stole | stolen |
| To find (encontrar) | found | found |
| To sell (vender) | sold | sold |
| To write (escrever) | wrote | written |
| To spend (gastar) | spent | spent |
| To eat (comer) | ate | eaten |
| To tell (contar) | told | told |
| To sit (sentar) | sat | sat |
| To catch (pegar) | caught | caught |

**1.** Traduza o diálogo.

– Did you buy a skateboard?

– No, I didn't buy a skateboard.

– What did you buy then?

– I bought a bicycle.

3. sentava, sentou

4. encontrava, encontrou

5. pagava, pagou

6. contava, contou, dizia, disse

7. vendia, vendeu

8. enviava, enviou

9. comprava, comprou

10. conhecia, conheceu, sabia, soube

**2.** Preencha a cruzadinha com estes verbos em inglês no **past tense**.

1. roubava, roubou

2. gastava, gastou

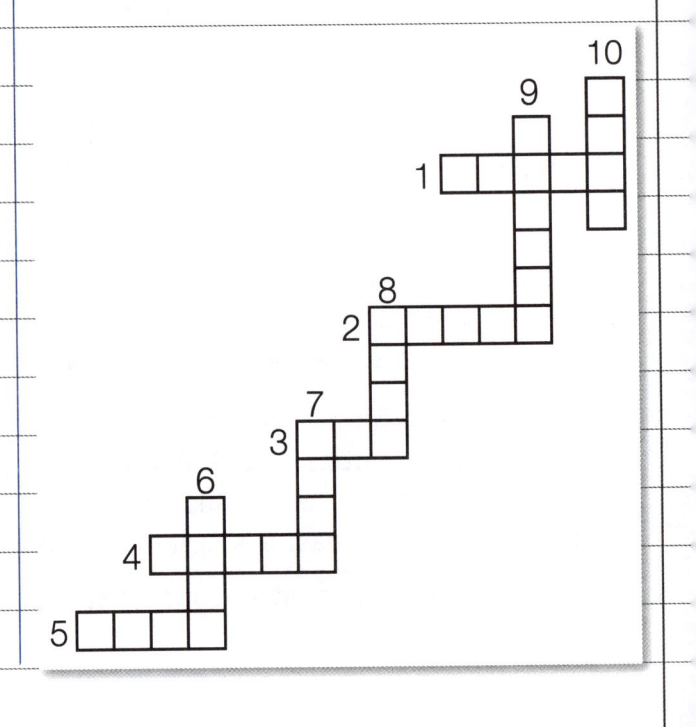

**3.** Mude para o **past tense**. Observe o exemplo.

Milton knows many countries.
**Milton knew many countries.**

a) We send a telegram.

b) He always pays the bill.

c) They buy and sell cars.

d) Francis always tells the truth.

e) She spends a lot of money on clothes.

f) We sit in front of the teacher.

g) She steals little objects.

h) My mother finds everything.

**4.** Escreva as frases na forma negativa. Observe o exemplo.

Milton knows many countries.
**Milton doesn't know many countries.**

a) She sent a telegram.

b) John paid the bill.

c) They bought a new house.

d) Francis told the truth.

e) She spent a lot of money on clothes.

f) John sat in front of me.

g) She stole little objects.

h) My mother found everything.

**5.** Escreva **short answers** (respostas curtas) afirmativas. Observe o exemplo.

Do you know my father?
Yes, I do.

a) Does she know England?

b) Did you pay the bill?

c) Did you find the keys?

**6.** Escreva **short answers** negativas. Observe o exemplo

Did you find her purse?
No, I didn't.

a) Does she know England?

b) Did you buy flowers?

c) Did you buy magazines?

d) Does she know Paris?

e) Did you pay the bill?

**7.** Siga os modelos e responda.

Do you buy magazines? (books)
No, I don't buy magazines.
I buy books.
Did she buy magazines? (books)
No, she didn't buy magazines.
She bought books.

a) Did you send a letter to Jane? (an e-mail)

b) Does your teacher tell stories? (jokes)

**8.** Observe as figuras e responda às questões.

a) What did the monkey do? (ate bananas)

b) Did Jane write a letter? (yes)

e) What did the waiter take to the girl? (orange juice)

c) What did he eat at dinner? (salad)

**9.** Responda às perguntas no tempo presente. Observe o exemplo.

to sell – sold – sold: vender
fruit and vegetables
What does a greengrocer sell?
**A greengrocer sells fruit and vegetables.**

a) to build – built – built: construir
houses, bridges and buildings
What does an engineer build?

d) Did Charles buy a red car? (No)

b) to cut – cut – cut: cortar
   women's hair
   What does a hairdresser do?

c) take care – took care – taken
   care: cuidar
   our health
   What does a doctor do?

d) take care – took care – taken
   care: cuidar
   our teeth
   What does a dentist do?

e) take care – took care – taken
   care: cuidar
   our pets, dogs, cats, birds
   What does a veterinarian do?

**10.** Encontre no caça-palavras o **past tense** destes verbos.

to sell — to buy
to find — to spend
to pay — to know
to steal — to see
to go — to write
to eat — to read
to sit — to speak
to take — to sleep
to tell

| T | O | O | K | O | O | L | S | Y | K | N | E | D |
|---|---|---|---|---|---|---|---|---|---|---|---|---|
| L | M | N | Z | E | Q | O | P | D | X | S | A | W |
| W | E | F | O | U | N | D | L | I | E | S | H | R |
| E | L | M | C | C | O | U | S | V | R | A | E | S |
| S | S | E | W | K | M | V | Y | K | I | T | B | K |
| W | O | Z | X | J | T | O | L | D | R | U | E | H |
| V | L | N | M | L | A | D | I | E | S | C | A | W |
| S | D | B | R | U | F | H | L | L | W | K | M | V |
| S | V | R | A | T | O | E | S | P | O | K | E | U |
| Q | L | I | H | X | S | B | S | U | B | B | R | U |
| S | L | E | P | T | Y | A | T | L | O | S | V | R |
| K | J | L | L | M | C | C | O | R | T | V | B | N |
| M | D | L | A | T | E | H | L | U | P | A | I | D |
| K | O | Z | X | J | H | O | E | B | R | U | E | H |
| N | B | N | M | L | A | D | N | E | S | C | A | W |
| E | B | S | P | E | N | T | L | L | W | K | M | V |
| W | B | N | M | L | A | D | I | E | S | C | A | W |
| K | J | L | C | A | W | C | B | O | U | G | H | T |
| K | J | L | L | M | C | R | O | R | T | V | B | N |
| Q | W | R | O | T | E | E | O | U | B | B | R | U |
| W | O | Z | X | J | H | A | B | B | R | U | E | H |
| Q | L | I | H | X | S | D | O | U | W | E | N | T |

# Lesson 12 – Personal pronouns

Leia com atenção os diálogos a seguir.

This gift is for **you**.

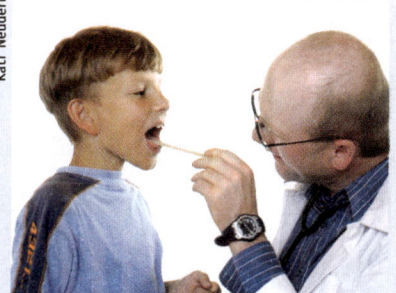

Show **me** your tongue.

**He** likes postcards.
Send **him** this one.
**It** is very beautiful.

### PERSONAL PRONOUNS

| Subject pronouns (Pronomes sujeitos) | Object pronouns (Pronomes objetos) |
|---|---|
| **I** (eu) | **me** (me) |
| **you** (tu, você) | **you** (te) |
| **he** (ele) | **him** (lhe, o) |
| **she** (ela) | **her** (lhe, a) |
| **it** (ele, ela) | **it** (lhe, o, a) |
| **we** (nós) | **us** (nos) |
| **you** (vós, vocês) | **you** (vos) |
| **they** (eles, elas) | **them** (lhes, os, as) |

Observe as frases:

a) I sent   **her**       an e-mail.
      obj. indireto + obj. direto
   (Eu enviei a ela    um e-mail.)

b) I sent    **an e-mail to her.**
      obj. direto   + obj. indireto
   (Eu enviei um e-mail     para ela.)

**Dialogue**
– Tomorrow is Sofia's birthday. I'm going to give **her** this perfum.
– Good idea! She's going to love **it**!

**1.** Traduza o diálogo acima.

**2.** Complete os diálogos com pronomes objetos.

a) – Next week is Helen's birthday. Let's give _____ a present?
   – What about a blouse?
   – Good idea! She likes clothes. She is going to love _____

b) – Next Friday is Jane and
Meg's birthday.
Let's give _____ a present?
– Meg and Jane like to read.
Let's give _____ books?
– It's a very good idea!

c) – Next month is my birthday.
What are you going to
give _____ ?
– What about a surfboard?
– Marvelous idea! I'm going to
remember _____ forever!

**3.** Traduza os diálogos do exercício anterior.

a)

b)

c)

**4.** Substitua os nomes por pronomes pessoais. Observe o exemplo.

Fred is waiting for Kate in front of the movies.
He is waiting for her in front of the movies.

a) Does **the teacher** like **the students**?

b) Can you give **these flowers** to **Nanci**?

c) **Suzi** loves **George**.

d) **George** loves **Suzi**.

e) **The newsagent** sells **newspaper and magazines**.

f) **The football players** run after the ball.

**5.** Reescreva as frases, mudando a posição do pronome objeto. Observe o exemplo

I am going to give a present to you.

**I am going to give you a present.**

a) I am going to give you a present.

b) We can buy a toy to him.

c) The office boy delivers documents to them.

d) The teacher explained you the problem.

e) She paid the bill to me.

**Observação:**

Bookshop: livraria (UK)
Bookstore: livraria (USA)

**6.** Complete as sentenças com **me, it, her**.

a) – Please give an apple to _____

b) – Oh, this blouse is very nice! How much is it?
   – _____ costs 10 dollars.

c) – Please give _____ this book. She must read it. _____ is very interesting.

**7.** Complete as frases abaixo com pronomes pessoais.

a) – Who are _____ ?
   – I am Paul Goldman.

b) She is singing. Listen to _____ .

c) – Here is your coffee.
   – Thank _____ very much.

d) – Excuse _____ , sir. Can you tell _____ where Palm Street is?

e) Flavia likes Robert. She often goes to the movies with _____ .

f) The bird is singing. Look at _____ in that tree.

g) – Where did you buy this book?
   – I bought _____ in a bookshop downtown.

h) Those girls are very nice. We like _____ very much.

i) – Do you like your parents?
   – Yes, I like _____ very much.

j) – Does Mary like you?
   – No, she doesn't like _____ .
   – She likes Peter.

**8.** Escolha o pronome pessoal correto e complete as frases.

a) her – she
   I go to school with _____ every day.

b) we – us
   She sits near _____ .

c) her – she
   I meet _____ at school every day.

d) he – him
   Don't give _____ any money.

e) she – her
   I love _____ very much.

f) them – they
   I want to talk to _____ .

g) we – us
   The teacher explained the lesson to _____ .

h) he – him

I am sending an e-mail to          .

i) they – them

I invited          to the party.

j) she – her

She is an excellent student.
All the teachers like          .

k) it – he

Get your book.
Open          on page ten.

**9.** Substitua as palavras em destaque por pronomes oblíquos (**object pronouns**). Observe o exemplo.

Mary loves **John**.
**Mary loves him.**

a) James offered **flowers** to the teacher.

b) I cleaned **the room** in the morning.

c) Did you like **the film**?

d) They washed **the hands** with cold water.

e) I helped **my sister** yesterday.

f) Did you take **your books**?

g) I saw **Peter** yesterday.

h) I invited **John and Mary** to the party.

i) I sent **Margaret** some flowers.

j) I helped **my mother** in the kitchen.

**Observação:**

**After prepositions use the object pronouns.**

(Depois de preposições, use o pronome oblíquo.)

**10.** Escolha a alternativa correta.

a) The tourists send me postcards.
   Some of _____ send me postcards.
   ( ) they     ( ) them
b) Come with _____.
   ( ) I     ( ) me
c) She is playing tennis with _____.
   ( ) he     ( ) him
d) What can I do for _____?
   ( ) he     ( ) her

**11.** Mude a posição do objeto indireto.

a) I send the money **to him**.
b) She brings the gift **to John**.
c) I send some money **to my brother**.
d) She gives the money **to him**.
e) We give **John** the gift.
f) Show **Mark** the house.
g) Take **her** these flowers.

**12.** Riddle. Name me and you break me.

# Dictation

**13.** Ouça com atenção o ditado que o professor vai apresentar e escreva.

# Review – Lessons 10, 11 and 12

**Mom:** **Did you sell** your bicycle, George?
**George:** Yes, **I sold** it.
**Mom:** How much did you get?
**George:** 80 dollars!
**Mom:** 80 dollars! A nice amount! But why **did you sell** it?
**George:** I **didn't have** money and I wanted to give a present to my grandmother.
**Mom:** What **did you give** her?
**George:** I **gave** her a beautiful watch.

**1.** Traduza o diálogo acima.

**2.** Substitua as palavras em destaque pelo pronome pessoal objeto correspondente. Observe o exemplo.

I saw **Mary** on the street yesterday.
**I saw her on the street yesterday.**

a) I saw **your brother** at the movies last week.

b) Peter sent **Flavia** some flowers.

c) I go to work with **John and Fred** every day.

d) Put **the book** on the table.

e) I saw **the President** on TV last night.

f) Put **the money** in a bank.

g) You can go with **Jane** to the party.

h) I told **the teachers** about the accident.

i) Do you speak to **the tourists** in English?

j) Did you meet **your friends** at the party?

k) I wrote **your telephone number** in my notebook.

**3.** Passe as frases para o passado. Observe o exemplo.

I work at home.
**I worked at home.**

a) We live in São Paulo.

b) She cooks dinner for two people.

c) She cleans the room in the morning.

d) I am going to visit Jane at night.

e) They use a pen to write.

f) They prefer to go home.

g) They are moving to Rio.

**4.** Reescreva as frases, empregando os verbos no passado. Observe o exemplo.

They (arrive) late yesterday.
**They arrived late yesterday.**

a) We (work) hard until six o'clock.

b) She (dance) all night.

c) We (visit) our friends last week.

d) I (wash) my car last Saturday.

e) Finally she (finish) her work.

f) I (call) the doctor yesterday morning.

**5.** Escreva as frases na forma interrogativa. Observe o exemplo.

John came to class late.
**Did John come to class late?**

a) They knew my teacher.

b) They went to school.

c) They bought a new car last week.

d) She began a new course last month.

e) They drank whiskey at the party.

f) They found the documents in a bar.

**6.** Escreva as frases na forma negativa. Observe o exemplo.

She waited for me.
**She didn't wait for me.**
(ou **She did not wait for me.**)

a) We talked to Peter.

b) The teacher explained the lesson.

c) The dog barked last night.

d) We liked the film.

e) I worked in an office.

f) We entered the house.

g) She invited many friends.

h) I accepted the invitation.

# Additional texts

**ABOUT FRIENDSHIP**

A friend is always prepared to help you.
A friend is not selfish.
A friend is a good listener.
A friend does not lie to you.
A friend shares his problems with you.
A friend is patient.
A friend is not jealous of your success.
A friend understands what you are thinking.

**1.** Responda às questões.

   a) Leia e traduza os provérbios sobre a amizade.

   b) Escolha uma das frases dos provérbios do texto "About Friendship" e escreva abaixo:

**WHAT'S ON TV?**
**George:** What's on TV, Paul?
**Patty:** I don't know, George.
**George:** Let's see the program...
**Patty:** Wow! There is a cowboy film at 8 o'clock.
**George:** Look! At 9:30 there is a football match: Corinthians *versus* Flamengo. I can't miss that!
**Patty:** What's on next?
**George:** At 11 o'clock there is a comedy program with Renato Aragão.
**Patty:** Fantastic! I like him. He is very funny.

**2.** Responda às questões sobre o texto acima.

a) Who is speaking with Patty?

b) Patty and George are speaking about:
( ) school.   ( ) TV programs.
( ) a picnic. ( ) football matches.

c) What kind of film is on TV at 8 o'clock?

d) What is on TV at 9h30?

e) Patty likes Renato Aragão because:
( ) he is intelligent.
( ) he is very funny.
( ) he is nice.

f) Escreva **true** (verdadeiro) ou **false** (falso) de acordo com o texto:

( ) George and Patty intend to watch TV programs.
( ) The football match TV program begins at 10 o' clock.
( ) Patty likes Renato Aragão's comedy.

**3.** Agenda

> What day is today? Let me see my agenda. Oh! Today is Friday. Good! Tomorrow is Saturday.

Agora escreva em inglês, no espaço abaixo, a sua agenda semanal.

**INTERVIEWING A POLITICIAN**

Nelson is a newspaper reporter and today he is interviewing a politician about his occupation.

**Nelson:** Who are you?
**Man:** I am David Benson.
**Nelson:** What is your job?
**Man:** I am a politician.
**Nelson:** Are you happy with your job?
**Man:** Of course I am! Politics is a very interesting occupation!
**Nelson:** Thank you very much.

**4.** Responda às perguntas sobre o texto.

a) What is Nelson's occupation?

b) What is Nelson doing?

c) What is Benson's occupation?

d) Is Benson happy with his job?

**FIRE PREVENTION WEEK**

We need to prevent fires. It is our duty.
But how can we prevent fires?
Here are some good advices:

- Turn off the stove when you leave the house.
- Keep lighters and matches away from children.
- Keep alcohol and other fuels away from the stove.
- Don't leave wires uncovered.
- Don't play with fire.
- Write the Fire Department telephone in your notebook.
- If there is a fire, call the firemen immediately.
- If there is a fire, leave the house immediately.
- Don't run if your clothes catch fire. Roll on the ground.

**5.** Traduza o texto "Fire Prevention Week", reflita a respeito e discuta com os colegas sobre acidentes com fogo.

Many of the stadiums above are being reformed and new ones are being built for the World Football Cup in Brazil in 2014.

**6.** Responda de acordo com o texto.

a) What is the most popular sport in the world?

b) Where are football fans?

c) What do supporters take to the stadiums?

**FOOTBALL**

Football is the most popular sport in Brazil and in the world.

Football fans are in all countries. A festive atmosphere reigns among the supporters, who take flags, drums and firecrackers to the stadiums.

We have huge football stadiums in Brazil: Maracanã, in Rio; Morumbi, in São Paulo; Beira-Rio, in Porto Alegre; Mineirão, in Belo Horizonte; Arruda, in Recife; Serra Dourada, in Goiás, etc.

Maracanã stadium is one of the biggest in the world. It has a capacity of 100.000 people.

Today there are many teams of football with girls as players.

**7.** Escreva **true** (verdadeiro) ou **false** (falso) de acordo com o texto.

a) (     ) Today there are a lot of football teams of girls as players.

b) (     ) Football isn't popular in Brazil.

c) (     ) We have huge football stadiums in Brazil.

**8.** About you.

a) Where are you from?

b) What is your favorite football team? What team do you support?

c) Do you go to the stadium taking the flag of your team?
( ) Yes, I do.
( ) Sometimes I do.
( ) No, I don't.

> **SPORTS**
>
> **Daniel:** Do you like sports, Paul?
> **Paul:** Yes, I do. I like sports very much.
> **Daniel:** What are your favorite sports?
> **Paul:** My favorite sports are football, volleyball, basketball, handball and tennis.
> **Daniel:** And your sister Jane, what are her favorite sports?
> **Paul:** My sister prefers running, cycling and swimming.
> **Daniel:** Are sports important to you?
> **Paul:** Oh, no doubt. Sports give us more energy for physical and mental tasks and they are a great enjoyment of life.

**9.** Responda de acordo com o texto.

a) Ligue de acordo com o texto.

| | |
|---|---|
| | • volleyball |
| | • swimming |
| Paul's favorite sports are | • basketball |
| | • football |
| | • running |
| | • tennis |
| Jane's favorite sports are | • handball |
| | • cycling |

b) What are the benefits of sports?

**10.** Observe the example.

– My name is Alberto Moreno. I am twenty years old. I live in Buenos Aires, Argentina, at 203, Calle del Plata. I am an Argentinean college boy.

**PERSONAL INFORMATION**

This is Diana Silva. She is twenty-five years old. She lives in Rio de Janeiro, Brazil, at 158, Torres Av.
Diana is a Brazilian singer.

Family Name:   Silva
First Name:    Diana
Age:           18
Nationality:   Brazilian
Residence:     Rio de Janeiro
Address:       Av. Torres, 158
Occupation:    Singer

Family Name:
Name:
Age:
Nationality:
Residence:                 (city)              (country)
Address:
Occupation:

Agora, preencha a ficha ao lado com os dados do Alberto.

**DRUGS**

The world is facing a drug crisis. It's a very serious problem.

There are many campaigns against drugs. Each campaign has a message. For example: "JUST SAY NO!!", "CHOOSE LIFE, NOT DRUGS!", "STOP THE MADNESS!".

There are more drug-addicts today than before.

Here is what happens to drug-addicts:
**They destroy their health,
lose their friends,
hurt their families,
steal money.**

**11.** Responda de acordo com o texto.

a) What does it happen to drug-addicts?

b) Are there more drug-addicts today than before?

c) Are drugs a serious problem?

d) Escreva algumas mensagens para a campanha contra as drogas.

**ON SEPTEMBER 21$^{ST}$**

Arbor Day (Tree Planting Day)
The Arbor Day was first celebrated in the state of Nebraska, USA, in 1872. The idea of setting one day apart for planting trees began with Mr Sterling Morton. More than a million trees were planted in Nebraska the first year. Today the Arbor Day is commemorated all over the world on different dates, mainly in schools, with conversations about forests, soils, wildlife parks and recreation areas.

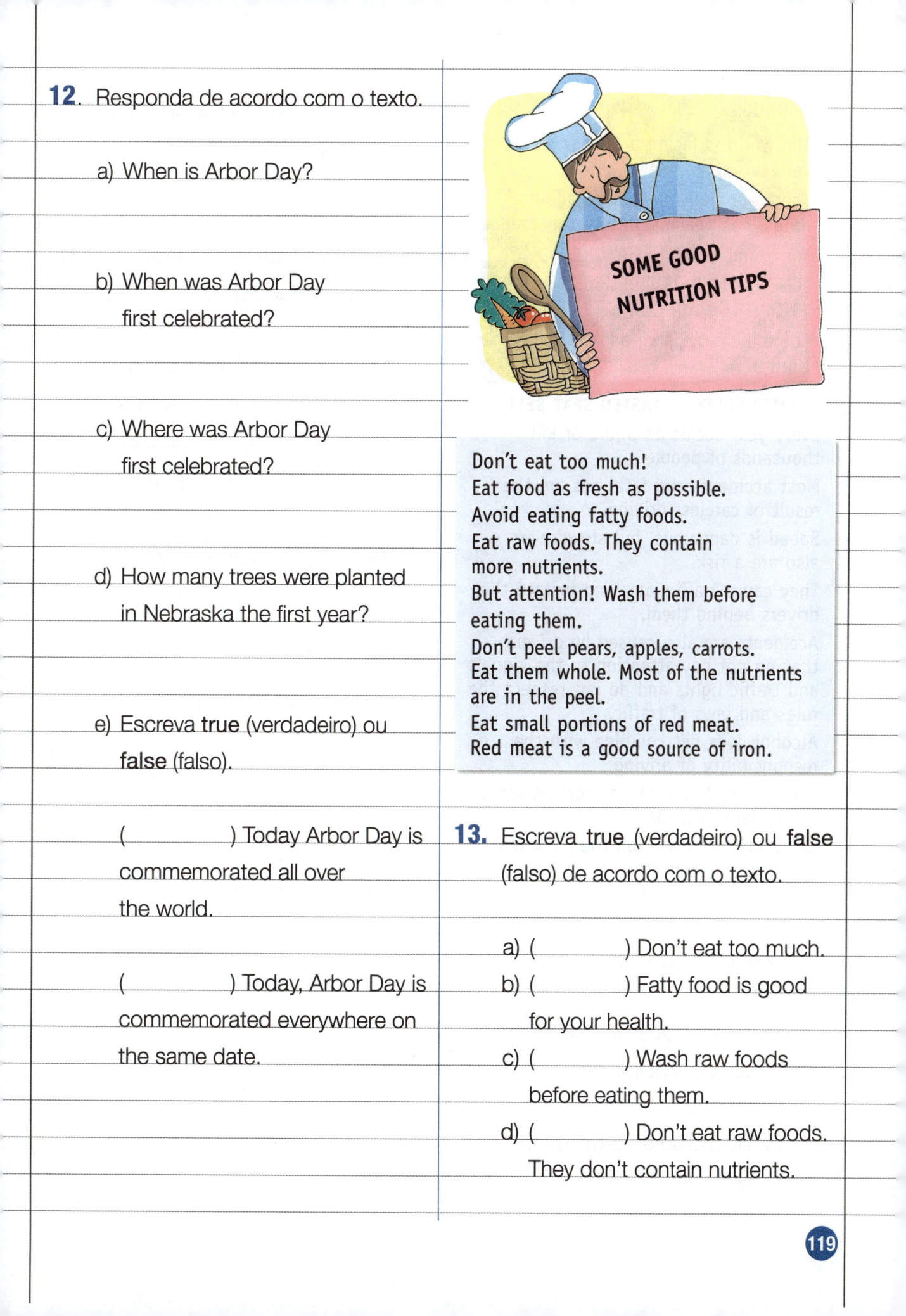

**12.** Responda de acordo com o texto.

a) When is Arbor Day?

b) When was Arbor Day first celebrated?

c) Where was Arbor Day first celebrated?

d) How many trees were planted in Nebraska the first year?

e) Escreva **true** (verdadeiro) ou **false** (falso).

(　　　) Today Arbor Day is commemorated all over the world.

(　　　) Today, Arbor Day is commemorated everywhere on the same date.

**SOME GOOD NUTRITION TIPS**

Don't eat too much!
Eat food as fresh as possible.
Avoid eating fatty foods.
Eat raw foods. They contain more nutrients.
But attention! Wash them before eating them.
Don't peel pears, apples, carrots. Eat them whole. Most of the nutrients are in the peel.
Eat small portions of red meat.
Red meat is a good source of iron.

**13.** Escreva **true** (verdadeiro) ou **false** (falso) de acordo com o texto.

a) (　　　) Don't eat too much.

b) (　　　) Fatty food is good for your health.

c) (　　　) Wash raw foods before eating them.

d) (　　　) Don't eat raw foods. They don't contain nutrients.

**AUTO SAFETY – FASTEN SEAT BELT**

Every year accidents injure or kill thousands of people.

Most accidents and fatalities are the result of careless driving.

Speed is dangerous, but slowdrivers also are a risk.

They cause traffic jams and irritate the drivers behind them.

Accidents are also caused by drivers that do not pay attention to the signals and traffic lights and do not respect the rules and laws of traffic.

Alcohol does not combine with the responsibility of driving.

The seat belt is a very important safety component in a car.

Children must travel on the back seats and use seat belt, too.

**14.** Responda de acordo com o texto.

a) Is seat belt an important safety component in a car?

b) Must children travel on the back seats?

c) Does alcohol combine with the responsibility of driving?

**15.** Escreva **true** (verdadeiro) ou **false** (falso) de acordo com o texto.

a) (　　　) Every year accidents kill many people.

b) (　　　) The seat belt is not important.

Traduza o texto "Auto Safety".

**PROVERBS**

"Appearances often deceive."

"The greatest conqueror is he who conquers himself."

"One good mother is worth a hundred teachers."

"If you want a thing done well, do it yourself."

"Every man is the architect of his own fortune."

**ANOTAÇÕES**

**16.** Escolha um dos provérbios e traduza-o.

# Fun time
## (Divirta-se aprendendo)

**1.** There are eight things in the first drawing that are different from the second one. Can you spot them? Find out eight differences in the second picture.

**2.** Escolha a alternativa correta.

a) Football is
   ( ) a game.
   ( ) a job.
   ( ) a place.

b) Brazil is
   ( ) a nationality.
   ( ) a boy's name.
   ( ) a country.

c) March is
   ( ) a year.
   ( ) a month.
   ( ) a day.

d) A supermarket is
   ( ) a ship.
   ( ) a shop.
   ( ) a farm.

e) A kitchen is
   ( ) a classroom.
   ( ) an airport.
   ( ) a room.

f) Dinner is
   ( ) a place.
   ( ) a meal.
   ( ) an airplane.

g) A player is
   ( ) a sport.
   ( ) a person.
   ( ) a place.

h) A fly is
( ) a bird.
( ) an airplane.
( ) an insect.

**NEW PARTS IN A MOTORCYCLE SHOP**

**The customer**: When I bought a motorcycle from you a few weeks ago, you said that your shop replaced anything broken.

**The motorcycle salesman**: Yes. What can I do for you? What parts do you need?

**The customer**: Well, I want a left eye, an ear, four teeth, a rib and a nose.

**3.** Mark the parts that the customer wants to replace.

( ) wheels     ( ) a nose
( ) an eye     ( ) motorcycle
( ) shoes     ( ) a rib
( ) an ear     ( ) teeth

**4.** Em cada coluna há uma palavra estranha ou intrusa (**odd**). Descubra-a e copie-a abaixo das tabelas.

| Numbers | Colors | Animals |
|---|---|---|
| Three | Yellow | Cow |
| Four | Blue | Horse |
| Two | Black | Cat |
| Six | White | Train |
| Nine | Green | Dog |
| Shirt | Eleven | |

| Sports | School | Food |
|---|---|---|
| Ball | Book | Ice cream |
| Soccer | Page | Pop corn |
| Football | Bicycle | Pencil |
| Father | Lesson | Rice |
| Cycling | Reading | Beans |

| Family | Clothes |
|---|---|
| Father | Tie |
| Sister | Shirt |
| Green | Shorts |
| Mother | Ice cream |
| Brother | Hat |

**5.** Encontre no labirinto as palavras positivas abaixo.

> life – love – success – happiness
> future – health – faith – ideal
> brightness – energy – enthusiasm
> friendship

```
S M D C L I F E C N C S A Z B
J M K L L B D M L O V E I F G
F I D E A L I O T H K I M D B
V D F G A X F A I T H E D C J
C V F R I E N D S H I P V L K
E N T H U S I A S M R I G O M
J D C E N E R G Y I J G T J S
M C H E R I N Q I E F G S B M
D F R T S U C C E S S M F N Y
B S I M I O F U T U R E K B I
N H A P P I N E S S U K O L A
J E R F H E A L T H S D A V O
S C I O I B R I G H T N E S S
```

**6.** Encontre no labirinto as palavras negativas.

> unhappiness – death – depression
> drugs – vices – darkness – degradation
> troubles – sorrow – loneliness

```
S V E U N H A P P I N E S S A
N C T R O U B L E S G J R D Q
A S D R U G S B N I M I O K F
V B D R A S O R R O W V R B H
B Z A E G D V I C E S V M J
V A L D E A T H B O I B F R K
M L O N E L I N E S S N U M V
C R E M A D I D L C I O M D M
R D E P R E S S I O N R U E B
L N M Y D A R K N E S S M B W
D E G R A D A T I O N I G J Z
```

**7.** Traduza o texto abaixo.

It's a question of choice.
Choose life, not drugs!
Just say NO to drugs!

**8.** Nature is life! Draw a landscape in the space below: a mountain, a river, birds in the sky, trees, a road, the sun and a house.

**9.** Escreva em inglês.

a) Uma bela paisagem.

Escreva em português.

b) Life in contact with nature makes us healthy.

**10.** A Thinking Game

a) Which of the things below can you wear?
Mark "1"

b) Which of the pictures below shows someone having trouble?
Mark "2"

c) Which of the pictures below shows something used in rainy days?
Mark "3"

( ) a coat          ( ) flying kite          ( ) the package tore

( ) an umbrella     ( ) a lamp              ( ) a car with a flat tire

**11.** About music.

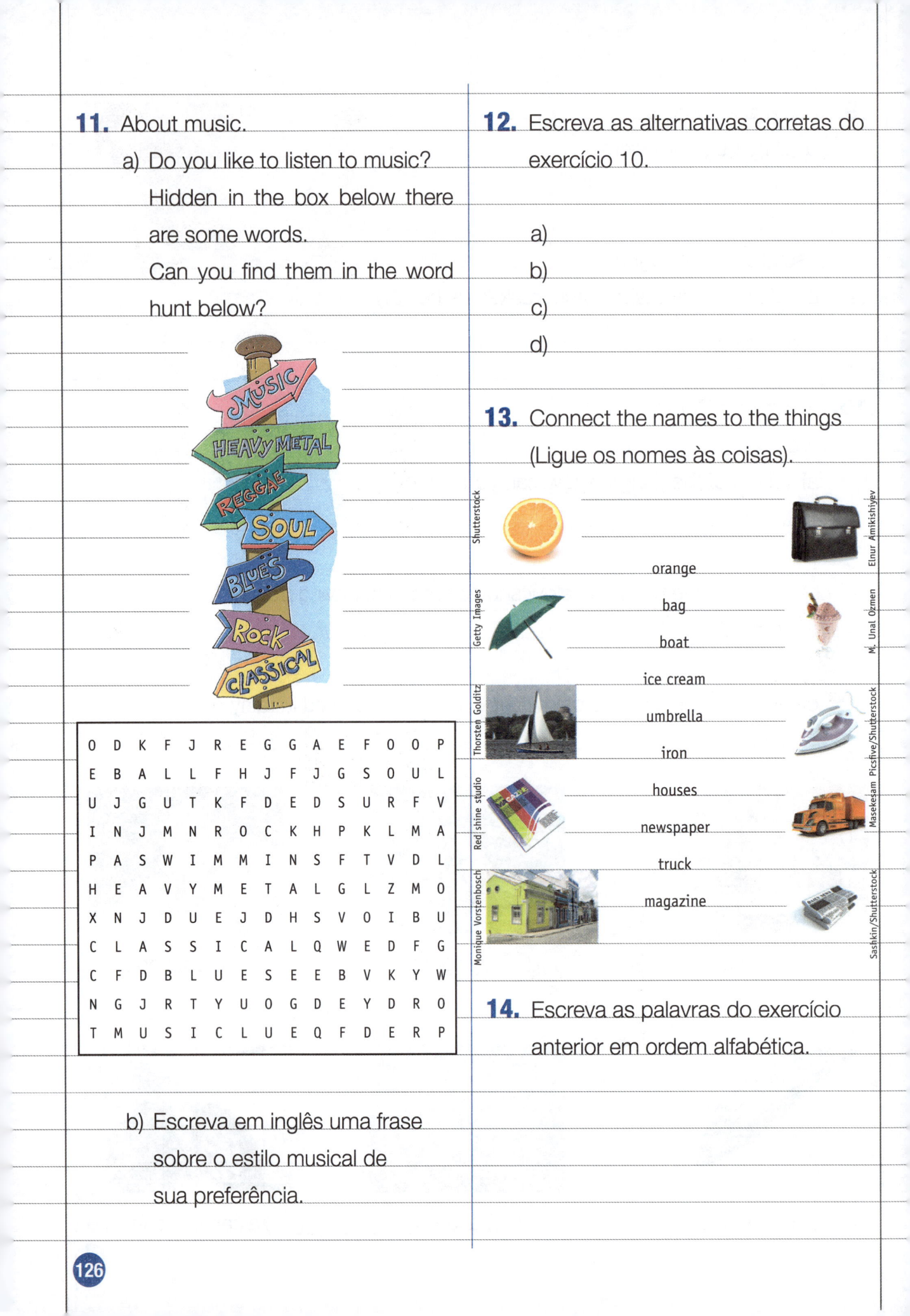

a) Do you like to listen to music? Hidden in the box below there are some words.

Can you find them in the word hunt below?

| O | D | K | F | J | R | E | G | G | A | E | F | O | O | P |
|---|---|---|---|---|---|---|---|---|---|---|---|---|---|---|
| E | B | A | L | L | F | H | J | F | J | G | S | O | U | L |
| U | J | G | U | T | K | F | D | E | D | S | U | R | F | V |
| I | N | J | M | N | R | O | C | K | H | P | K | L | M | A |
| P | A | S | W | I | M | M | I | N | S | F | T | V | D | L |
| H | E | A | V | Y | M | E | T | A | L | G | L | Z | M | O |
| X | N | J | D | U | E | J | D | H | S | V | O | I | B | U |
| C | L | A | S | S | I | C | A | L | Q | W | E | D | F | G |
| C | F | D | B | L | U | E | S | E | E | B | V | K | Y | W |
| N | G | J | R | T | Y | U | O | G | D | E | Y | D | R | O |
| T | M | U | S | I | C | L | U | E | Q | F | D | E | R | P |

b) Escreva em inglês uma frase sobre o estilo musical de sua preferência.

**12.** Escreva as alternativas corretas do exercício 10.

a)

b)

c)

d)

**13.** Connect the names to the things (Ligue os nomes às coisas).

orange

bag

boat

ice cream

umbrella

iron

houses

newspaper

truck

magazine

**14.** Escreva as palavras do exercício anterior em ordem alfabética.

**15.** Complete o começo ou o final de cada palavra.

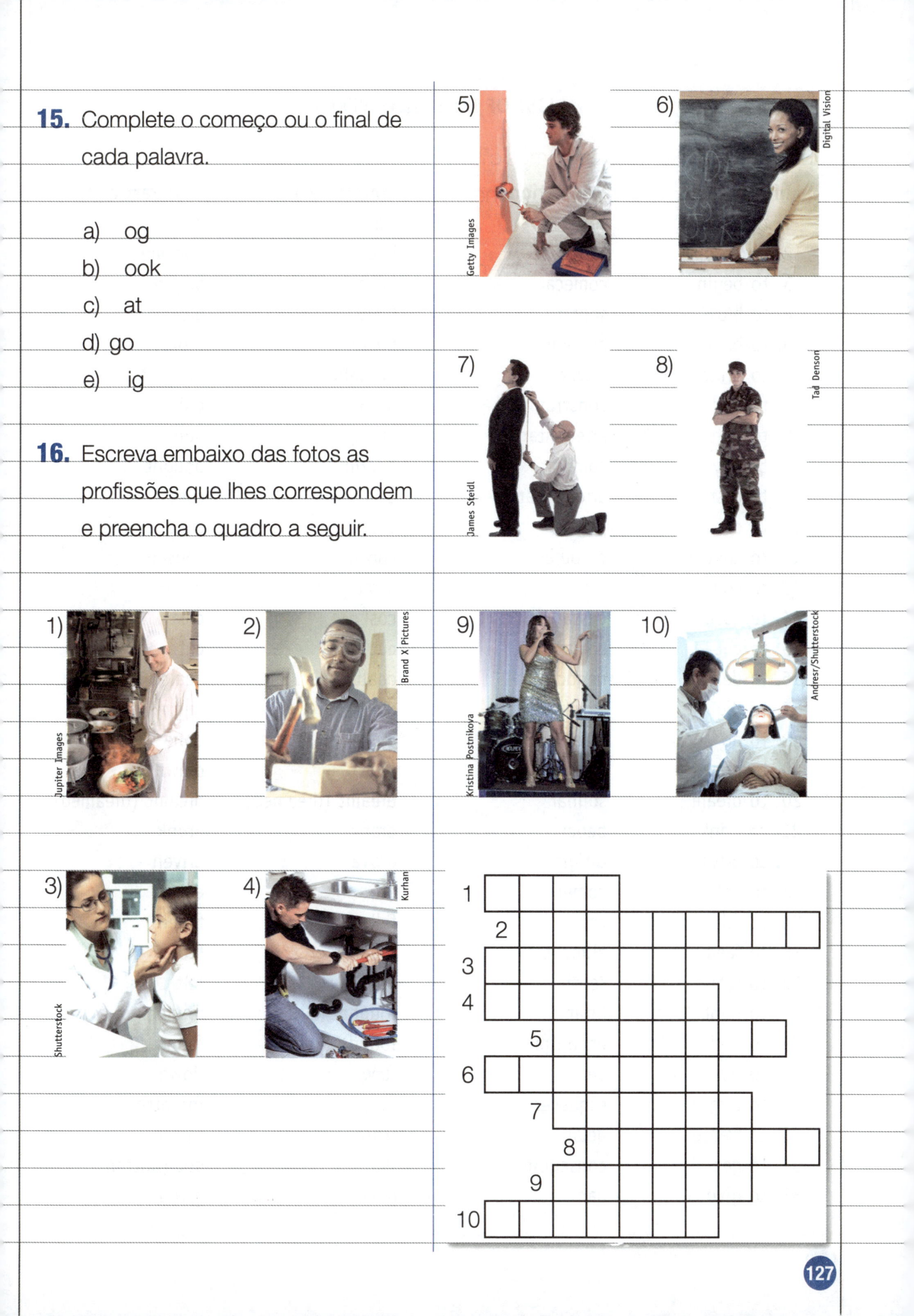

a) ___ og
b) ___ ook
c) ___ at
d) go ___
e) ___ ig

**16.** Escreva embaixo das fotos as profissões que lhes correspondem e preencha o quadro a seguir.

## LIST OF IRREGULAR VERBS

| Infinitive | Translation | Simple Past | Past Participle |
|---|---|---|---|
| 1. to be | ser, estar | was, were | been |
| 2. to become | tornar-se | becam e | become |
| 3. to begin | começar | began | begun |
| 4. to blow | soprar | blew | blown |
| 5. to break | quebrar | broke | broken |
| 6. to bring | trazer | brought | brought |
| 7. to build | construir | built | built |
| 8. to burst | arrebentar | burst | burst |
| 9. to buy | comprar | bought | bought |
| 10. to cast | arremessar | cast | cast |
| 11. to catch | pegar | caught | caught |
| 12. to choose | escolher | chose | chosen |
| 13. to come | vir | came | come |
| 14. to cost | custar | cost | cost |
| 15. to cut | cortar | cut | cut |
| 16. to deal | negociar | dealt | dealt |
| 17. to dig | cavar | dug | dug |
| 18. to do | fazer | did | done |
| 19. to draw | desenhar | drew | drawn |
| 20. to dream | sonhar | dreamt (dreamed) | dreamt (dreamed) |
| 21. to drink | beber | drank | drunk |
| 22. to drive | dirigir | drove | driven |
| 23. to eat | comer | ate | eaten |
| 24. to fall | cair | fell | fallen |
| 25. to feed | alimentar | fed | fed |
| 26. to feel | sentir | felt | felt |
| 27. to fight | lutar | fought | fought |
| 28. to find | encontrar | found | found |
| 29. to fly | voar | flew | flown |
| 30. to forget | esquecer | forgot | forgotten |
| 31. to freeze | gelar | froze | frozen |
| 32. to get | conseguir | got | got (gotten) |
| 33. to give | dar | gave | given |

| | | | |
|---|---|---|---|
| 34. to go | ir | went | gone |
| 35. to grow | crescer | grew | grown |
| 36. to hang | pendurar | hung | hung |
| 37. to have | ter | had | had |
| 38. to hear | ouvir | heard | heard |
| 39. to hide | esconder | hid | hidden |
| 40. to hit | bater | hit | hit |
| 41. to hold | segurar | held | held |
| 42. to hurt | machucar | hurt | hurt |
| 43. to keep | guardar | kept | kept |
| 44. to know | saber | knew | known |
| 45. to lay | pôr, deitar | laid | laid |
| 46. to lead | guiar | led | led |
| 47. to learn | aprender | learnt (learned) | learnt (learned) |
| 48. to leave | deixar, partir | left | left |
| 49. to lend | emprestar | lent | lent |
| 50. to let | deixar, permitir | let | let |
| 51. to lie | mentir, jazer | lay | lain |
| 52. to light | iluminar | lit (lighted) | lit (lighted) |
| 53. to lose | perder | lost | lost |
| 54. to make | fazer, fabricar | made | made |
| 55. to mean | significar | meant | meant |
| 56. to meet | encontrar-se com | met | met |
| 57. to pay | pagar | paid | paid |
| 58. to put | pôr | put | put |
| 59. to read | ler | read | read |
| 60. to ride | cavalgar | rode | ridden |
| 61. to ring | tocar a campainha | rang | rung |
| 62. to rise | erguer-se | rose | risen |
| 63. to run | correr | ran | run |
| 64. to say | dizer | said | said |
| 65. to see | ver | saw | seen |
| 66. to sell | vender | sold | sold |
| 67. to send | enviar | sent | sent |
| 68. to set | colocar, fixar | set | set |
| 69. to shake | sacudir | shook | shaken |
| 70. to shine | brilhar | shone (shined) | shone (shined) |

| | | | |
|---|---|---|---|
| 71. to shoot | atirar, disparar | shot | shot |
| 72. to show | mostrar | showed | shown (showed) |
| 73. to shut | fechar | shut | shut |
| 74. to sing | cantar | sang | sung |
| 75. to sink | afundar | sank | sunk |
| 76. to sit | sentar | sat | sat |
| 77. to sleep | dormir | slept | slept |
| 78. to slide | escorregar | slid | slid |
| 79. to slit | fender, rachar | slit | slit |
| 80. to smell | cheirar | smelt | smelt |
| 81. to speak | falar | spoke | spoken |
| 82. to speed | apressar-se | sped (speeded) | sped (speeded) |
| 83. to spend | gastar | spent | spent |
| 84. to spoil | estragar | spoilt | spoilt |
| 85. to spread | espalhar | spread | spread |
| 86. to spring | saltar | sprang | sprung |
| 87. to stand | ficar de pé | stood | stood |
| 88. to steal | roubar | stole | stolen |
| 89. to strike | bater | struck | struck |
| 90. to swear | jurar | swore | sworn |
| 91. to sweep | varrer | swept | swept |
| 92. to swim | nadar | swam | swum |
| 93. to swing | balançar | swung | swung |
| 94. to take | tomar | took | taken |
| 95. to teach | ensinar | taught | taught |
| 96. to tell | contar, dizer | told | told |
| 97. to think | pensar | thought | thought |
| 98. to throw | arremessar | threw | thrown |
| 99. to understand | entender | understood | understood |
| 100. to wake | acordar | woke | woken |
| 101. to wear | vestir, usar | wore | worn |
| 102. to wed | desposar | wed (wedded) | wed (wedded) |
| 103. to wet | umedecer | wet | wet |
| 104. to win | ganhar, vencer | won | won |
| 105. to wring | espremer, torcer | wrung | wrung |
| 106. to write | escrever | wrote | written |

# General vocabulary

**A**

**a**: um, uma
**a day**: por dia
**a lot of**: muito, muitos, uma porção
**abandoned**: abandonado
**abbey**: abadia
**about**: sobre, a respeito de
**above**: acima de
**absent**: ausente
**accept**: aceitar
**acceptance**: aceitação
**accident**: acidente
**across**: através de
**advantage**: vantagem
**advice**: conselho
**afraid of**: com medo de
**after**: depois de
**afternoon**: tarde
**against**: contra
**age**: idade
**agency**: agência
**ago**: atrás, antes
**air**: ar
**airplane**: avião
**airport**: aeroporto
**alive**: vivo
**all**: tudo, todo, todos
**all night long**: a noite toda
**all over the world**: em todo o mundo
**all right**: tudo bem, bem
**alone**: sozinho
**along**: ao longo de
**aloud**: em voz alta
**also**: também
**always**: sempre
**am**: sou, estou
**among**: entre (muitos)
**amount**: quantia
**an**: um, uma
**ancient**: antigo
**and so on**: e assim por diante
**angry**: bravo, furioso
**another**: outro
**answer**: responder, resposta
**answered**: respondeu
**any**: algum, nenhum
**anything**: algo, nada
**apartment** (USA): apartamento
**appearance**: aparência
**apple**: maçã
**appointment**: encontro
**approximately**: aproximadamente
**April**: abril
**architect**: arquiteto, artífice
**are**: são, estão
**area**: área
**ark**: arca
**arrested**: preso
**arrive**: chegar
**as**: como

**as fresh as**: tão fresco quanto
**as usually**: como de costume
**ask**: pedir, perguntar, fazer
**asked**: perguntou
**at**: à, no, na, em
**at home**: em casa
**at night**: à noite
**at school**: na escola
**at six**: às seis
**at the doctor's**: no consultório médico
**ate**: comi, comeu, comemos...
**atomic bomb**: bomba atômica
**attend**: frequentar
**attention**: atenção
**August**: agosto
**aunt**: tia
**auto safety**: segurança no carro
**avenue**: avenida
**award**: prêmio
**away**: longe, embora

**B**
**baby**: bebê
**back seat**: assento traseiro
**bad**: ruim
**badly**: mal
**bag**: mala
**baker**: padeiro
**ball**: bola
**balloon**: balão
**bank**: banco

**bar**: bar
**barber's**: barbeiro (at the barber's: na barbearia)
**bark**: latir
**basket**: cesta
**bat**: bastão, porrete, taco
**bath**: banho
**battle**: batalha, luta
**be**: ser, estar
**beach**: praia
**bean**: feijão
**beautiful**: bonito
**because**: porque
**become**: tornar-se
**bed**: cama
**bedroom**: quarto
**been**: sido, estado
**beer**: cerveja
**before**: antes, antes de
**beg**: pedir
**began**: começou
**beggar**: pedinte
**begin**: começar
**behalf**: em defesa de, em nome de (on behalf of)
**behind**: atrás de
**believe**: acreditar, crer
**bell**: campainha, sino
**belong**: pertencer
**below**: abaixo de
**belt**: cinto

**benefit:** benefício
**better:** melhor
**between:** entre
**beware:** tenha cuidado
**beyond:** além de
**Bible:** Bíblia
**bicycle:** bicicleta
**big:** grande
**bill:** conta
**bird:** pássaro
**birth:** nascimento
**birthday:** aniversário
**black:** preto
**blind:** cego
**block:** quadra
**blond:** loiro
**blonde:** loira
**blouse:** blusa
**blue:** azul
**boat:** barco
**body:** corpo
**bone:** osso
**book:** livro
**bookseller:** livreiro
**bookshop:** livraria
**boring:** chato, enjoado
**born:** nascido (was born: nasceu)
**borrow:** pedir emprestado
**both:** ambos
**bottle:** garrafa
**bought:** comprou, comprei

**box:** caixa
**boy:** menino, rapaz
**boyfriend:** namorado
**branch:** galho
**bread:** pão
**break:** quebrar
**breakfast:** desjejum, café da manhã
**bridge:** ponte
**bright:** brilhante
**brightness:** claridade, brilho
**broke:** quebrou
**broken:** quebrado
**brother:** irmão
**brown:** marrom
**brush:** escovar, escova
**build:** construir
**building:** construção, prédio, edifício
**bus:** ônibus
**but:** mas
**butcher:** açougueiro
**butcher´s:** açougue
**butter:** manteiga
**buy:** comprar
**by:** por, de, por meio de
**by bus:** de ônibus
**by means of:** por meio

**C**

**cabbage:** repolho
**cage:** gaiola
**cake:** bolo

**call**: chamar, telefonar
**called**: chamou, chamado, chamei
**came**: vieram
**camera**: máquina fotográfica
**campaign**: campanha
**camping**: acampamento
**can**: pode, podemos, podem
**can't**: não posso, não pode
**cards**: baralho, cartas
**care**: cuidado
**careless**: falta de cuidado
**carnation**: cravo (flor)
**carpenter**: carpinteiro
**carpet**: carpete
**carrot**: cenoura
**carry**: carregar
**cart**: carroça
**cat**: gato
**catch**: pegar, agarrar, prender
**cauliflower**: couve-flor
**cause**: causar, causa
**celebrate**: comemorar
**celebrated**: comemorando
**chair**: cadeira
**change**: mudar
**cheap**: barato
**cheese**: queijo
**chef**: chefe
**chemist**: farmacêutico
**child**: criança, filho
**children**: crianças, filhos

**choice**: escolha
**choose**: escolha, escolher
**Christmas**: Natal
**church**: igreja
**cigar**: charuto
**cigarette**: cigarro
**cinema**: cinema
**city**: cidade
**claim**: reclamar
**class**: aula
**classical music**: música clássica
**classroom**: sala de aula
**clean**: limpar, limpo
**cleaned**: limpou
**(vacuum) cleaner**: aspirador de pó
**clerk**: balconista, atendente de balcão
**climb**: subir
**close**: fechar
**cloth**: pano
**clothes**: roupas
**clown**: palhaço
**coast**: costa
**coat**: paletó
**coffee**: café
**cold**: frio
**college**: universidade, faculdade
**colony**: colônia
**comb**: pente, pentear
**come**: vir
**come back**: voltar
**come back home**: voltar para casa

**come in:** entrar
**comfort:** conforto
**coming:** vindo
**complain:** queixar
**compose:** compor
**computer:** computador
**confess:** confessar
**conqueror:** conquistador
**conquer:** conquistar
**consider:** considerar
**contact:** contato
**contain:** conter
**convoke:** convocar
**cook:** cozinheiro, cozinhar
**cookery:** cozinha, culinária
**cookies:** biscoitos
**copy:** copiar
**corner:** canto, esquina
**corrupt:** corrupto
**cost:** custar, custa
**correct:** correto, corrigir
**could:** podia, poderia
**couldn't:** não podia
**country:** país, campo
**course:** curso (of course: certamente, com certeza)
**cover:** cobrir
**cow:** vaca
**cowboy:** vaqueiro
**criminal:** criminoso, bandido
**crisis:** crise

**crowd:** multidão
**crowded:** apinhado, cheio de gente
**cry:** chorar, gritar
**crying:** chorando
**cup:** xícara
**customs:** costumes
**cut:** cortar
**cycling:** ciclismo

**D**

**dance:** dançar, dança
**dangerous:** perigoso
**darkness:** escuridão, trevas
**date:** data, encontro
**daughter:** filha
**day:** dia
**dead:** morto
**deaf:** surdo
**dear:** querido
**death:** morte
**deceive:** enganar
**December:** dezembro
**decide:** decidir
**deep:** profundo
**degradation:** degradação
**deliver:** entregar
**deluge:** dilúvio
**dentist:** dentista
**desk:** carteira
**destroy:** destruir
**diamond:** diamante

**dictation**: ditado
**die**: morrer
**difference**: diferença
**different**: diferente
**difficult**: difícil
**difficulty**: dificuldade
**dinner**: jantar
**direction**: direção
**dirty**: sujo
**disappointed**: desapontado, frustrado
**discover**: descobrir
**discuss**: discutir
**dish**: travessa, prato
**disobey**: desobedecer
**distant**: distante
**do**: fazer
**do not, don't**: não
**doctor**: médico, doutor
**doctor's**: consultório médico
**document**: documento
**does**: faz
**does not, doesn't**: não
**dog**: cão
**doll**: boneca
**done**: feito, realizado
**door**: porta
**door-keeper**: porteiro
**doubt**: dúvida
**down**: baixo, debaixo
**downtown**: centro da cidade
**dozen**: dúzia

**draw**: desenhe, desenhar
**drawer**: gaveta
**drawing**: desenho, desenhando
**dream**: sonhar
**dress**: vestido, vestir-se
**drink**: beber, bebida
**drive**: dirigir
**driver**: motorista
**driving**: dirigindo
**drop**: cair, derrubar
**drug**: droga
**drug-addict**: viciado em drogas
**drugstore**: farmácia, drogaria
**drum**: tambor
**dumb**: mudo
**during**: durante
**duty**: dever

**E**

**each**: cada
**early**: cedo
**earn**: ganhar
**easy**: fácil
**eat**: comer
**egg**: ovo
**eight**: oito
**eighty**: oitenta
**eighth**: oitavo
**electrical device**: equipamento elétrico
**electrician**: eletricista
**electricity**: eletricidade

**employ**: empregar
**e-mail**: correio eletrônico
**engaged**: engajado, comprometido
**engineer**: engenheiro
**England**: Inglaterra
**English**: inglês
**enjoy**: aproveitar, usufruir, gozar
**enjoyment**: prazer, alegria, diversão
**enough**: bastante, suficiente
**enter**: entrar
**environment**: meio ambiente
**escape**: escapar
**establish**: estabeleceram
**evening**: tardezinha, noite
**ever**: sempre
**every**: cada, todos
**every day**: cada dia, todos os dias
**everything**: tudo
**exact**: exato
**exactly**: exatamente
**exam**: exame
**examine**: examinar
**exciting**: excitante, vibrante
**exercise**: exercício
**exist**: existir
**expensive**: caro
**explain**: explicar
**explained**: explicou, explicado
**eye**: olho

**F**

**facing**: encarando, enfrentando
**factory**: fábrica
**fair**: bonito, feira
**faith**: fé
**family**: família
**famous**: famoso
**fan**: fã
**far**: longe
**far from**: longe de
**farm**: fazenda
**farmer**: fazendeiro
**fast**: rápido
**fasten**: apertar
**fat**: gordo
**father**: pai
**fatty**: gorduroso
**favourite (Br.), favorite (Am.)**: favorito
**feed**: alimentar
**feel**: sentir
**feet**: pés
**fellow**: colega
**fence**: cerca
**few**: poucos
**field**: campo
**fifteen**: quinze
**fifty**: cinquenta
**fight**: brigar, lutar
**fill in**: preencher, completar
**film**: filme
**finally**: finalmente

**find**: encontrar
**finish**: terminar, acabar
**fire**: fogo
**fireman**: bombeiro
**firm**: firma **first**: primeiro
**fish**: peixe, peixes
**fishmonger**: peixeiro
**fishmonger's**: peixaria
**fix**: consertar
**flag**: bandeira
**flat (Br.), apartment (Am.)**: apartamento
**flood**: inundar
**floor**: assoalho, piso
**florist**: florista
**flower**: flor
**fly**: voar; mosca
**food**: alimento, comida
**foot**: pé
**for**: para, por
**for ever**: para sempre
**for example**: por exemplo
**for her**: para ela
**for him**: para ele
**foreign**: estrangeiro
**forest**: floresta
**forever**: para sempre
**forgave**: perdoou
**forget**: esquecer
**forgive**: perdoar
**form**: formulário
**fortune**: fortuna

**free**: livre; grátis
**free time**: tempo livre
**freedom**: liberdade
**frequently**: frequentemente
**fresh**: fresco
**Friday**: sexta-feira
**fridge**: geladeira
**friend**: amigo
**friendship**: amizade
**from**: de, desde
**from here**: daqui
**fruit**: fruta, frutas
**fuel**: combustível
**fun**: diversão, brincadeira
**funny**: engraçado, cômico
**furious**: furioso
**furiously**: furiosamente
**furniture**: mobília, móveis

## G

**game**: jogo
**garage**: garagem
**garden**: jardim
**gave**: dei, deu, deram
**general**: geral
**generally**: geralmente
**german**: alemão
**get**: pegar, chegar, conseguir, comprar
**get up**: levantar
**ghost**: fantasma, espírito
**ghost office**: correio dos fantasmas

**gift**: presente
**girl**: garota, menina
**girlfriend**: namorada
**give**: dar, dê
**give up**: desistir
**glad**: alegre
**glass**: copo, vidro
**glasses**: copos, óculos
**go**: ir
**go away**: ir embora
**go out**: sair
**goal**: gol, objetivo
**goalkeeper**: goleiro
**God**: Deus
**goes**: vai
**going**: indo (I'm going: eu vou)
**gold**: ouro
**golden**: de ouro, dourado
**good**: bom
**goodbye**: até logo
**goods**: mercadorias
**grade**: grau, série
**grammar**: gramática
**grandmother**: avó
**grandparent**: avô, avó
**grandparents**: avós
**grass**: grama
**great**: grande, ótimo
**greatest**: o maior
**green**: verde
**greengrocer**: verdureiro

**ground**: chão
**gun**: arma

# H

**had**: tinha, teve
**had to**: tinha de
**hair**: cabelo
**hairdresser**: cabeleireiro
**half**: meio, metade
**hand**: mão
**happen**: acontecer
**happened**: aconteceu
**happiness**: felicidade
**happy**: feliz
**hard**: árduo, duro, arduamente
**hardly**: dificilmente
**has to**: tem de
**hat**: chapéu
**hate**: odiar, detestar
**have**: ter, tem
**have to**: ter de
**health**: saúde
**healthy**: saudável
**hear**: escutar
**heard**: escutei
**heavy**: pesado
**he's gone out**: ele saiu
**help**: ajudar
**help him**: ajudá-lo, ajude-o
**hen**: galinha
**her**: dela, lhe, a, a ela, seu, sua

**here**: aqui
**here it is**: aqui está
**hers**: dela
**hi**: oi
**high**: alto
**himself**: a si mesmo
**his**: dele, seu, sua
**history**: história
**holiday**: feriado, férias
**home**: casa, lar
**homeless**: sem casa
**homework**: trabalho doméstico, lição
**honey**: mel
**hope**: esperança
**horse**: cavalo
**hour**: hora
**house**: casa
**how**: como
**how heavy?**: que peso?
**how long?**: quanto tempo?
**how many?**: quantos?
**how many times?**: quantas vezes?
**how much?**: quanto?
**how often?**: com que frequência?
**how old are you?**: quantos anos você tem?
**how tall?**: que altura?
**hug**: abraçar
**huge**: enorme
**hundred**: cem
**hungry**: faminto, com fome
**hurry up**: apressar-se
**hurt**: machucar, ferir
**hut**: cabana

**I**

**I**: eu
**I'm going**: eu vou
**I was born**: eu nasci
**ice cream**: sorvete
**idea**: ideia
**if**: se
**immediately**: imediatamente
**imported**: importado
**improve**: melhorar
**in**: em
**in front of**: na frente de
**in the**: no, na, nos, nas
**in the afternoon**: à tarde
**in the morning**: de manhã
**industry**: indústria
**injure**: machucar, ferir
**inside**: do lado de dentro
**interesting**: interessante
**interview**: entrevista
**interviewing**: entrevistando
**into**: para dentro
**invitation**: convite
**invite**: convidar
**invited**: convidou
**in what**: naquilo
**iron**: ferro
**irritate**: irritar

**is**: é, está
**isn't she?**: não é (ela)? não está (ela)?
**it's**: ele é, ele está, ela é, ela está
**its**: seu, sua, dele, dela
**it's Bob's**: é de Bob
**it's hers**: é dela
**it's his**: é dele
**it's your turn**: é sua vez
**it's yours**: é seu

## J
**jam, traffic jam**: engarrafamento, congestionamento de trânsito
**jealous**: invejoso, ciumento
**jewel**: joia
**jeweller**: joalheiro
**jewelry store**: joalheria
**job**: emprego, trabalho
**joke**: piada, anedota
**joy**: alegria
**joyfully**: alegremente
**judge**: juiz
**jump**: pular
**jumping**: pulando
**just**: justo, mesmo, agora

## K
**keep**: manter, guardar
**key**: chave
**kill**: matar
**kind**: espécie, tipo; bondoso

**kiss**: beijo, beijar
**kitchen**: cozinha
**knife**: faca
**know**: conhecer, saber
**known**: conhecido

## L
**lake**: lago
**land**: terra, aterrisar, desembarcar
**landscape**: paisagem
**language**: língua
**large**: grande, vasto
**last**: último
**last time**: última vez
**late**: tarde, atrasado
**law**: lei
**lean**: magro
**learn**: aprender
**leave**: deixar, partir, sair
**left**: saiu, deixou, esquerda
**lemon**: limão
**lend**: emprestar
**length**: comprimento
**lesson**: lição, aula
**let's**: vamos
**let's go**: vamos
**letter**: carta
**level**: nível
**librarian**: bibliotecário
**library**: biblioteca
**lick**: lamber

**lie**: mentira, mentir
**life**: vida
**lift**: levantar; elevador; carona
**lighter**: isqueiro
**lights**: lâmpadas, luzes
**like**: gostar
**list**: lista
**listen to**: ouvir, escutar
**listener**: ouvinte
**little**: pouco, pequeno
**live**: morar, viver
**lived**: morou, viveu
**living room**: sala de estar
**loaf of bread**: filão de pão ("bengala")
**loaves of bread**: filões de pão ("bengalas")
**lock**: fechar (com chaves)
**London**: Londres
**loneliness**: solidão
**long**: longo, comprido, durante
**look**: olhar
**look after**: cuidar
**lose**: perder
**lost**: perdido
**loud**: alto (som, voz)
**lovely**: adorável, lindo
**low**: baixo
**lunch**: almoço, lanche

**M**

**madam**: madame, senhora
**madness**: loucura

**magazine**: revista
**maid**: empregada
**mail**: correio, postar no correio
**mainly**: principalmente
**make**: fazer, fabricar
**mall**: shopping
**man**: homem
**manager**: gerente
**many**: muitos
**March**: março
**marine**: marinha
**market**: mercado, feira
**married**: casou
**marry**: casar
**marvelous**: maravilhoso
**masked**: mascarado
**match**: partida; fósforo, ligar
**mathematics (maths)**: matemática
**may**: pode, podem
**May**: maio
**meal**: refeição
**mean**: significar
**meaning**: significado
**meat**: carne
**medicine**: remédio
**meet**: encontrar
**memory**: memória
**men**: homens
**merchandise**: mercadoria
**merry**: alegre, feliz
**mess**: bagunça, sujeira

**message**: mensagem
**met**: encontrei, encontrou
**midday**: meio-dia
**middle**: metade
**milk**: leite
**mine**: meu(s), minha(s)
**minute**: minuto
**mirror**: espelho
**miss**: senhorita; perder, faltar
**mistake**: erro
**moderation**: moderação
**modern**: moderno
**Monday**: segunda-feira
**money**: dinheiro
**monkey**: macaco
**month**: mês
**moon**: lua
**more**: mais
**morning**: manhã
**most**: a maioria
**mother**: mãe
**motorcycle**: moto
**mountain**: montanha
**mouse**: rato
**mouth**: boca
**move**: mudar, mover
**movies**: cinema
**Mrs**: senhora
**much**: muito
**multiply**: multiplicar
**mum (Br.), mom (Am.)**: mãezinha, mamãe

**museum**: museu
**must**: precisa, precisam
**mustn't**: não deve
**my**: meu(s), minha(s)
**myself**: eu mesmo, a mim mesmo

# N

**nail**: unha; prego
**name**: nome
**nature**: natureza
**nave**: marinha
**near**: perto de
**need**: precisar de
**nest**: ninho
**never**: nunca
**new**: novo
**news**: notícia, notícias, novidades
**newsagent**: jornaleiro
**newspaper**: jornal
**newsstand**: banca de jornais
**next**: próximo, a seguir
**nice**: bonito, bom, bacana
**night**: noite
**no**: não, nenhum
**Noah**: Noé
**Nobel Prize**: Prêmio Nobel
**nobody**: ninguém
**noisy**: barulhento
**none**: nenhum
**north**: norte
**not**: não

**notebook:** agenda, caderno de anotações
**now:** agora
**now and then:** de vez em quando
**nurse:** enfermeira
**nutrition:** nutrição

## O

**obey:** obedecer
**occupations:** profissões
**occur:** ocorrer
**oceam:** oceano
**of:** de
**of course:** naturalmente
**off:** fora
**offend:** ofender
**offer:** oferecer
**office:** escritório
**office-boy:** ajudante de escritório
**officer:** oficial, funcionário
**often:** frequentemente
**oil:** óleo, petróleo
**old:** velho
**on:** sobre
**on foot:** a pé
**on time:** a tempo, dentro do horário
**on the way:** no caminho
**on TV:** pela televisão
**once:** certa vez, uma vez
**once a week:** uma vez por semana
**once a year:** uma vez por ano
**only:** somente

**open:** abrir, aberto
**opening:** abrindo
**opportunity:** oportunidade
**or:** ou
**orange:** laranja
**order:** ordem, encomendar
**other:** outro
**our:** nosso
**out:** fora
**out of:** fora de
**outside:** do lado de fora
**over:** acima de
**over there:** lá, ali
**own:** próprio

## P

**packet:** pacote
**paid:** pagou
**paint:** pintar, pintura
**painter:** pintor
**palace:** palácio
**paper:** papel, jornal
**pardon:** perdão
**parents:** pais (pai e mãe)
**park:** parque, estacionar
**parking lot:** estacionamento
**Parliament:** Parlamento
**party:** festa
**past tense:** tempo passado
**pay:** pagar
**pay attention:** prestar atenção

**peace**: paz
**pear**: pêra
**pedestrian**: pedestre
**peel**: descascar
**pen**: caneta
**pencil**: lápis
**pen-friend**: amigo por correspondência
**people**: pessoas, povo
**perceive**: perceber
**person**: pessoa
**pet**: animal de estimação
**phone**: telefone, telefonar
**photo**: foto
**pick up**: colher
**picnic**: piquenique
**picture**: quadro, pintura, figura
**pig**: porco
**piece**: pedaço
**pill**: pílula
**pilgrim**: peregrino
**place**: lugar
**plane**: avião
**plant**: plantar
**plate**: prato
**play**: jogar
**player**: jogador
**playing**: jogando, brincando
**please**: por favor
**pleasure**: prazer
**plug**: plugue, pino
**pocket**: bolso

**point**: ponto, apontar, mostrar
**police**: polícia
**police station**: delegacia
**policeman**: policial
**politician**: político
**politics**: política
**pollution**: poluição
**poor**: pobre
**popcorn**: pipoca
**porter**: carregador
**post office**: correio
**postcard**: cartão postal
**postman (Br.), mailman (Am.)**: carteiro
**pot**: pote
**potato**: batata
**pound**: libra (453 gramas)
**pound**: libra (moeda inglesa)
**practice**: praticar
**prefer**: preferir
**prepare**: preparar
**prevent**: prevenir
**prevention**: prevenção
**principal**: principal, diretor
**private**: privado, particular
**proclaim**: proclamar
**program**: programa
**promise**: prometer
**pull**: puxar
**pullover**: pulôver
**pupil**: aluno
**purse**: bolsa

**put**: pôr
**put on**: vestir, pôr sobre

## Q
**quality**: qualidade
**quantity**: quantidade
**quarter**: quarto (fracionário)
**question**: pergunta
**quick**: rápido
**quickly**: rapidamente

## R
**rain**: chuva, chover
**raise**: levantar, criar
**rascal**: malandro, velhaco
**raw**: cru
**reach**: alcançar, chegar
**read**: ler
**real**: real, verdadeiro
**really**: realmente
**receive**: receber
**record**: registro, gravação
**recreation**: recreação, lazer
**red**: vermelho
**red-haired**: ruiva(o)
**reference**: referência
**refuse**: recusar
**reign**: reinar, reino
**religious**: religioso
**remember**: lembrar-se
**repair**: consertar

**reply**: responder, retrucar
**reprimand**: repreender
**requires**: requer, exige
**respect**: respeito, respeitar
**result**: resultado
**return**: voltar
**rice**: arroz
**rich**: rico
**right**: direito, direita
**rights**: direitos
**ring**: anel; tocar campainha
**risk**: risco
**river**: rio
**road**: estrada, rua
**rob**: roubar
**rock music**: rock (música)
**roll**: rolar
**room**: sala, cômodo
**rubbish**: lixo
**rule**: regra, norma
**ruler**: régua
**run**: correr
**running**: correndo, corrida

## S
**sad**: triste
**safety**: segurança
**said**: disse
**sail**: velejar, navegar
**sailor**: marinheiro
**sale**: venda

**salesman**: vendedor
**salt**: sal
**same**: mesmo
**sand**: areia
**sandwich**: sanduíche
**sank**: afundou
**satisfied**: satisfeito
**Saturday**: sábado
**save**: salvar, economizar
**saw**: viu
**say**: dizer, diga
**school**: escola
**schoolmate**: colega de escola
**score**: marcar
**scorn**: desprezo
**sea**: mar
**search**: procurar
**season**: estação
**seat**: assento, sede
**seat belt**: cinto de segurança
**second**: segundo
**Second World War**: Segunda Guerra Mundial
**secret**: segredo
**see**: ver, veja
**seem**: parecer
**selfish**: egoísta
**sell**: vender
**seller**: vendedor
**send**: enviar
**sent**: enviou, enviado, enviaram
**serious**: sério

**serve**: servir
**set**: colocar, estabelecer
**set apart**: separar, destacar
**setting**: colocando, estabelecendo
**settle**: estabelecer
**settlement**: assentamento
**settler**: colono
**several**: vários
**several times a day**: várias vezes por dia
**severe**: severo
**share**: dividir, compartilhar
**shelf**: prateleira
**she is going to pay**: ela vai pagar
**shining**: brilhando
**ship**: navio
**shirt**: camisa
**shoes**: sapatos
**shop**: loja, fazer compras
**shop window**: vitrine
**shopkeeper**: lojista
**shopping center**: centro de compras
**short**: curto, pequeno, baixo
**shorts**: short, calção
**shout**: gritar
**show**: mostrar, espetáculo
**shower**: chuveiro, banho de chuveiro
**shut**: fechar
**sick**: doente
**sign**: assinar
**signal**: sinal
**simplify**: simplificar

| | |
|---|---|
| **since**: desde | **sometimes**: algumas vezes |
| **sing**: cantar | **son**: filho |
| **singer**: cantor(a) | **song**: canção, música |
| **singing**: cantando | **soon**: logo, |
| **sink**: afundar | **soon after**: logo depois |
| **sister**: irmã | **sorrow**: tristeza |
| **sit**: sentar | **soup**: sopa |
| **sitting**: sentado, sentando | **source**: fonte |
| **skirt**: saia | **south**: sul |
| **sky**: céu | **Spanish**: espanhol |
| **sleep**: dormir | **speak**: falar |
| **slippery**: escorregadio | **speaker**: locutor, orador |
| **slow**: vagaroso | **speech**: discurso |
| **slow-driver**: motorista vagaroso | **speed**: velocidade |
| **slowly**: vagarosamente | **spend**: passar, gastar |
| **small**: pequeno | **spill**: derrubar |
| **smile**: sorrir, sorriso | **spilt**: derramou |
| **smoke**: fumar, fumaça | **spinach**: espinafre |
| **snake**: cobra | **spoke**: falou |
| **so**: tão, tanto, portanto | **spot**: aponte, marque |
| **so many**: tantos | **spread**: espalhar |
| **so much**: tanto | **spring**: primavera |
| **soccer**: futebol | **square**: quadrado, praça |
| **socket**: soquete | **stadium**: estádio |
| **socks**: meias | **stamp**: selo |
| **soil**: solo | **star**: estrela |
| **soldier**: soldado | **start**: começar |
| **solve**: resolver | **state**: estado |
| **some**: alguns | **station**: estação |
| **somebody**: alguém | **stationer**: vendedor de papelaria |
| **something**: algo, alguma coisa | **stationery store**: papelaria |

**stay**: ficar
**steak**: bife
**steal**: roubar
**still**: ainda
**stop**: parar, pare
**stories**: histórias
**story**: história
**stove**: fogão
**street**: rua
**strict**: severo
**strong**: forte
**study**: estudar
**subject**: assunto, matéria
**submarine**: submarino
**subway**: metrô
**success**: sucesso
**sugar**: açúcar
**sugar bowl**: açucareiro
**sun**: sol
**Sunday**: domingo
**sunny**: ensolarado
**sunshine**: brilho do sol
**supermarket**: supermercado
**support**: sustentar, apoiar
**supporter**: fã, torcedor
**sure**: certo, seguro
**sweep**: varrer
**sweet**: doce
**swim**: nadar
**swimming**: natação, nadando

**T**

**table**: mesa
**take**: pegar, levar, tomar
**talk**: conversar
**tall**: alto
**task**: tarefa
**tea**: chá
**teacher**: professor, professora
**teaches**: ensina
**team**: time
**teeth**: dentes
**telegram**: telegrama
**television**: televisão
**television set**: aparelho de televisão
**tell**: contar, dizer, falar
**tell the time**: dizer as horas
**tennis shoes**: tênis
**tenth**: décimo
**terrible**: terrível
**test**: teste
**text**: texto
**thank you**: obrigado
**thanks**: obrigado
**that**: aquele, aquela
**the biggest**: o maior
**their**: deles, delas
**theirs**: deles, delas
**them**: os, as, lhes
**then**: então, depois
**there**: lá
**there are**: há (plural)

**there is:** há (singular)
**there was:** havia (singular)
**there were:** havia (plural)
**these:** estes
**thief:** ladrão
**thin:** magro, fino
**thing:** coisa
**think:** pensar
**third:** terceiro
**thirsty:** sedento, com sede
**thirteen:** treze
**thirty:** trinta
**this:** este
**this way:** deste modo
**thought:** pensamento
**those:** aqueles
**thousand:** mil
**three times:** três vezes
**through:** através de
**Thursday:** quinta-feira
**ticket:** bilhete, passagem, entrada
**tie:** gravata
**time:** tempo
**times:** vezes
**tip:** dica
**tired:** cansado
**to:** para, a
**toast:** bronzear, torrar
**today:** hoje
**together:** juntos
**toilet:** toalete, banheiro

**tomorrow:** amanhã
**tongue:** língua
**tonight:** esta noite
**too:** demais; também
**too much:** demais
**took:** pegou, levou, pegamos
**top:** parte de cima, topo
**touch:** tocar
**tourist guide:** guia turístico
**tower:** torre
**town:** cidade
**toy:** brinquedo
**toy store:** loja de brinquedos
**toyshop:** loja de brinquedos
**traffic jam:** congestionamento de trânsito
**traffic lights:** semáforo
**train:** trem
**traitor:** traidor
**translate:** traduzir
**transportation:** transporte
**travel:** viajar
**treat:** tratar
**tree:** árvore
**trouble:** problema, perturbar
**trousers:** calça
**truck:** caminhão
**true:** verdadeiro
**truth:** verdade
**try:** tentar, experimentar
**Tuesday:** terça-feira
**turn:** virar, mudar, vez

**turn off**: desligar
**turn on**: ligar
**twenty**: vinte
**twice a week**: duas vezes por semana
**two**: dois

**U**
**ugly**: feio
**umbrella**: guarda-chuva
**uncle**: tio
**uncovered**: descoberto
**under**: debaixo de
**underline**: sublinhar
**understand**: compreender
**unfortunately**: infelizmente
**unhappiness**: infelicidade
**unhealthy**: sem saúde, doente
**universe**: universo
**until**: até
**up**: para cima
**use**: usar
**usually**: usualmente, geralmente

**V**
**vacation**: férias
**vegetable**: legume
**very**: muito
**very much**: muitíssimo
**vice**: vício
**village**: vilarejo

**W**
**wait**: esperar
**waiter**: garçom
**wakes up**: acordar
**walk**: caminhar
**wall**: parede, muro
**wallet**: carteira (de dinheiro)
**want**: querer, desejar
**war**: guerra
**warn**: avisar, advertir
**was**: era, estava, foi, fui
**was born**: nasceu
**wash**: lavar
**washed**: lavou, lavado
**watch**: assistir, relógio
**water**: água; regar
**way**: caminho, modo, maneira
**weak**: fraco
**wear**: usar (roupas), vestir
**wearing**: usando, vestindo
**weather**: tempo (estado atmosférico)
**Wednesday**: quarta-feira
**week**: semana
**weekend**: fim de semana
**well**: bem
**went**: foi, fui, fomos
**were**: foram, eram, foi
**what**: o que, qual
**What a good program!**: Que programa bom!
**What about?**: Que tal?
**What do you look like?**: Como você é? (geral)

**What do you look like?**: Como você é? (aparência)
**What did you do?**: O que você fez?
**What do you do?**: O que você faz?
**What for?**: Para quê?
**What fun!**: Que engraçado! Que divertido!
**What is Mario like?**: Como é o Mário?
**What is the matter?**: Qual é o problema? Qual é o assunto?
**what's**: o que é, o que está, qual é, qual está
**What time is it?**: Que horas são?
**What's on TV?**: O que está passando na TV?
**wheel**: roda; volante
**when**: quando
**where**: onde
**Where are you from?**: De onde você é?
**where's**: onde é, onde está
**Where were you?**: Onde você esteve?
**which**: qual, que
**white**: branco
**who**: quem, que
**whole**: inteiro
**whose**: de quem, cujo
**why**: por que
**why not**: por que não
**wide**: largo
**width**: largura
**wildlife**: vida selvagem
**window**: janela, vitrine
**wine**: vinho

**wire**: fio
**with**: com
**without**: sem
**without saying**: sem dizer
**woman**: mulher
**women**: mulheres
**women's**: das mulheres
**wonderful**: maravilhoso
**word**: palavra
**work**: trabalho, trabalhar, obra
**worker**: trabalhador, operário
**world**: mundo
**worth**: valioso, valor (It's worth: vale)
**write**: escrever
**wrong**: errado
**wrote**: escreveu

## Y

**year**: ano
**yellow**: amarelo
**yes**: sim
**yesterday**: ontem
**you are**: você é, você está, vocês são, vocês estão
**young**: jovem, novo
**yours**: seu(s), sua(s)
**yourself**: você mesmo

## Z

**zoo**: zoológico